The Smart Woman's Guide to Travel

Travel More. Travel Well. Travel Soon.

Vikki Walton

The Smart Woman's Guide to Travel

Copyright © 2018 by Vikki Walton

All rights reserved

No part of this publication may be reproduced, stored in a retrieval system or transmitted in any way by any means, electronic, mechanical, photocopy, recording, or otherwise, without the prior permission of the author except as provided by USA copyright law.

Formatted by Rik - Wild Seas Formatting
(http://www.WildSeasFormatting.com)

Dedicated
to

All the women who long for adventure.

Introduction

Maybe it's genetic. Or it's a need to venture beyond your current circumstances. For whatever reason, many people—and especially women—love to travel.

For those women who simple adore travel, the idea of travel for you is invigorating, exciting, and something you love to do.

Conversely, travel may seem like a far-off dream.

Either way, I'm here to help you achieve your vision to travel.

First, you'll understand how planning can turn a good trip into an extraordinary adventure. Next, you'll learn how to pick the best form of transportation and lodging that suits you and your desires best. You'll also discover how the activities you want to do will help you create your perfect trip.

You will be provided with some safety and health tips before and during your trip. And finally, you'll gain insights into how to travel more, travel well and travel soon!

Ready to get started?

First, let's begin with why you want to travel.

There are many reasons women love to travel.

Travel puts you there. If you're a life-long learner like me, there's nothing like standing where history occurred. Yes, in our technological age, you can read about it and see it on any number of visual screens any time you want. But seeing it in person is taking it to a whole other level. It can also change your perspective from what you've been taught.

Travel can test you.

The fact is, every day we get up and we go through our routine. We know it by rote. You'll be surprised to find that even the simple act of figuring out how to turn on an appliance in a new country becomes an adventure. Navigating from point A to B will take you out of your comfort zone. Immersion in different cultures can be challenging. Traveling with others or traveling alone can be a challenge. Travel forces you to confront things that bother you about others or yourself.

Yet, all those challenges are worth it!

You meet people that would never have crossed your path at home. People you meet and experiences you share become memories you will cherish all your life. On travels, I enjoy interacting with people of different cultures, religions, and political beliefs. These experiences affirm and enlighten my own opinions. For those I disagree with, it is a good reminder of practicing respect and self-control.

Travel can enchant you. You may find you fall in love. With yourself. Traveling solo can be one of the most empowering things you can do as a woman. Having to rely on yourself can be scary for some women. It's when you realize how genuinely capable you are is the moment when you recognize your worth and power. Of course, you don't have to travel to love yourself or to know your worth. It's just that for some women it is a way to instill more profound self-love.

Travels makes you appreciative. It makes you thankful of where you live and what you have. Far too often it is easy to take people and things in our life for granted. It is also a good reminder of things at home that might need changing.

Travel occurs for many reasons.

It could be that you want an adventure. It may be that you love the same daily routine which brings comfort and stability. But there is also incentive to break out and do something that has been a dream of yours for years.

It may be that you need an escape from a difficult time in your life to grieve or gain perspective. Agatha Christie writes in her biography that she needed to remove herself from the familiar. She had been dealing with the death of her mother, the monumental task of cleaning out her beloved home, Ashfield, ill health to the point of a nervous breakdown and the dissolution of her marriage.

Travel may be time to rest and relax away from the duties of home and work. Yes, it's a cliché but I'm noting it here that the adage of women's work is never done is true. For a woman, and especially for those who are mothers or care for others, there is no being away from work. You simply switch gears and move on to the next thing that needs doing. Going away is a time to recharge and to give yourself the gift of self-care.

It can be a time of bonding of couples, families, or friends. Some of my favorite trips have been with my daughters and my friends. Family trips instill memories that last beyond the moment. Couples that take time to get away can find their delight and desire for one another renewed.

You may seek to give back through volunteer efforts. Are you passionate about a particular area? There are so many ways that you can incorporate volunteering into vacation time.

Last, it could be a time of celebration. A significant birthday or achievement is worth celebrating.

What's your reason for traveling? What's your reason for not traveling more?

Now that you've recognized why you want to travel and why you don't travel more, let's dig a bit deeper into what often holds you back from traveling or that limits the enjoyment of your trips.

There are key areas that surround a trip. They are planning, transportation, accommodations, activities, safety and health. Let's talk about planning for a moment. Being spontaneous is fun if you have all the time and money in the world. However, planning can allow you to enjoy your trip without having to spend your time worrying about where you're going to spend the night. There's nothing as frustrating as driving all day only to find yourself exhausted and unable to get a hotel room because of a big event that weekend.

Planning also saves you time and money. Doing your research will help you uncover city passes that can provide you with travel on local public transportation and admittance into attractions. They often allow you to skip lines—thus saving you time—and may even include discounts with restaurants or other venues. In Chapter Two, you'll get some insights into what type of a planner you are and how to choose the best method for planning for your personality.

One of the things we never want to plan on is something bad happening. Unfortunately, bad things do and can happen. Some may be frustrating like your luggage not arriving at your destination for a day or two, others can be more devastating like being in a vehicle accident or having all your money stolen.

Therefore, it's imperative to prepare while anticipating that the well-thought-out scenario will probably not occur. Taking a pro-active approach ensures you that no matter where you go that you have done everything within your power to ensure your safety and welfare. You will find information on safety in Chapter Five.

While safety and security are a vital part of planning, they also extend to during and after your trip. The same can be said of your health. There's nothing that can ruin travel plans faster than becoming ill before, during or after your trip. You'll find information on health in Chapter Six.

Packing for your trip is another area where you need to adjust for your personality as well as your trip. Chapter Seven on packing is a short guide on how to haul less and enjoy your trip more.

We are a wired society. Technology can be useful, but it can also be detrimental. Use your technology wisely but don't allow it to distract from taking time to focus on that moment. The more you connect with your device for advice, the less you interact with people. In order to get a true sense of place, you need to connect with its population. Yes, you can find a restaurant online but why not ask someone on the street to recommend their favorite place? Chapter Eight will provide a bit of insight into how to stay in touch abroad.

This guide is divided into three sections.

The first section includes all the chapters about the various areas of your trip from planning to packing.

The second section is for your use. This is where you jot down travel information such as hotel addresses, confirmation codes, etc.

Yes, you can use your computer. But what happens years down the road and you can't remember that favorite bed and breakfast or restaurant. Even this planning section can become a great trip keepsake.

Finally, the last section is for your use on the trip. Memories fade quickly. Add that quick note at the end of the day. Include your favorite meal, embrace your artistic side and do a quick sketch of something that catches your eye.

Chapter One

Planning

Planning either strikes dread in your heart or fills you with a sense of purpose. In most cases, you will fall in one of these three categories:

The Meticulous Planner

You're someone who has every hour of your trip scheduled. You want to know where you're going, what you're doing and when, and how much it will cost. The idea of "winging it" makes you anxious.

The Partways Planner

You're someone who likes to create a skeleton foundation for your travel. You've got the transportation, lodging and essential activities locked down. But you've left room for serendipitous side trips or spur-of-the-moment adventures.

The Place Planner

You're someone who picks a place and sets out on an adventure. You haven't made reservations for lodging or have any specific activities in mind. You just go with an open mind and heart ready to enjoy the moment.

None of these types of planners are better or worse than the other ones. Each has its pros and cons. I, myself, fall in the Partways Planner. I pick the place I'm going, I know what I want to do, and this allows me to find deals on lodging, activities, etc. I don't like to pack the day so full that merely sitting and watching the world go by would not be on the schedule. But it all comes down to personality.

Let's start with the primary components for planning your next adventure. These are (in no particular order) your personality, those of any travel companions, destination and activity desires, as well as comfort level which also relates to budget.

Consider Your Personality

Are you an extrovert? If so, you may prefer trips that involve other people traveling with you. As an extrovert, your idea of a great vacation may be dancing until dawn or being in a fun crowd watching a concert. Interacting with others will increase your happiness while traveling so aim for group tours.

If you're an introvert, you may prefer sightseeing alone. Introverts will often enjoy solo travel or travel in a smaller group. An ideal day for an introvert might be a day lying in a beach chair reading your favorite author. It's not to say that an introvert wouldn't also enjoy dancing until dawn. But an introvert needs alone time to recharge while an extrovert needs people.

An ambivert (someone who exhibits both traits) will work well in many travel settings. Yet, most people tend to lean more towards a need for people or a need to be alone. You know yourself.

It's important to respect your personality when it comes to trips. Extroverts may do well with having a roommate or someone around. Whereas an introvert may need a room alone to have the space to recharge her batteries.

When traveling with companions, personality is an important factor to consider ensuring the success of the trip.

An easy way to determine your ideal trip for your personality is to list all the things that you want to do. Then go down the list and check off if you prefer to experience that activity alone or with others. You may check both if you're okay with either choice. Tally your list. You will have a score for solo events as well as with others. From the information, you'll discover if a solo or group trip, or one that combines the two is best.

Discover that you would prefer a solo trip? Many women (myself included) love solo trips. It's easy to connect with others by joining day group tours. You can also discover local groups that share your interests.

Destination Desires

Where have you always wanted to go?

Is any particular place calling to you?

Remember that where you may want to go is yours alone. First, decide where you want to go. Then, determine what you want to do. Eating some excellent gourmet food may be on your list or viewing a particular piece of art. Your idea of an ideal trip may be to spend the day shopping or even napping as a warm breeze caresses your face. Are you someone that likes to be active? Maybe a walking or hiking trip would suit you better than a bus tour.

Traveling solo? Consider creating a vision board. You can begin by collecting information in an online file or a travel box. Determine your top "must-dos."

Traveling as a group? Gather your friends or family together. Discuss what everyone wants to do on the trip. This discussion is a critical factor in designing a successful trip.

Determine Your Comfort Level

Your comfort level is all about your feelings of security. Would you be comfortable sleeping in a person's home or do you feel more secure in a chain hotel? Does the idea of taking the metro or subway fill you with dread or a sense of adventure? Lodging and transportation are two key areas to consider when planning for your experience.

Everyone has a comfort level.

One of the best things about traveling is learning to break out of your comfort level. Once you can give up some control, you will realize you can still be safe while experiencing more. Additionally, you'll find that you often save money-- a bonus!

Comfort impacts you on the emotional level as well as the physical level.

Make a list of various comfort level areas. Note which ones are of an emotional nature while others could be of a physical nature.

Here's an example.

If you are from an urban environment and regularly take public transportation, chances are that you will do well when using it in a foreign country.

If you have never used public transportation, not only may this cause you some emotional or mental angst, but it may impact your physical comfort as well.

Two areas where your comfort level will be apparent is the form of transportation you employ and the lodging you choose at your destination.

Transportation might include taking a taxi versus ride programs such as uber. You might choose public transportation instead of renting a vehicle. This is an excellent choice for urban areas. Of course, the least expensive transport is walking.

Taking public transportation will stretch your budget. It will also give you a more significant connection with the place you're visiting. Additionally, this is a great way to see places not on your list. However, for some individuals, walking in an unfamiliar neighborhood may trigger an uncomfortable feeling. In addition to the emotional component, walking could influence a person's physical comfort level if she is not used to much activity.

Lodging is another area where you can splurge or save money. Of any area, lodging plays a critical part in physical and emotional comfort levels. If you are uncomfortable around strangers, a hotel may be the way to maintain your comfort level. For those who consider strangers as friends they haven't met yet, bed and breakfasts and other similar establishments will be within your comfort zone.

Besides comfort level, an option may work better for specific trip portions. Will you be catching an early flight home? You may want to be in a hotel that is close to the airport that provides a free shuttle.

Comfort also has to do with physical care. Airlines continue to make seats smaller and closer together. Sitting six hours or more scrunched into an airplane seat may leave you with physical aches and pains. Yes, it may be a cheap flight but is it worth it if you arrive cranky with a backache?

Comfort should always be your first consideration in conjunction with convenience and cost. I'll share more about this in the chapters on transportation and lodging.

Once you have determined your personality, destination desires and your comfort level, the fun of planning can kick in to high gear. Of all the things that make a good trip great, the primary one is to create a trip theme.

Create A Theme

No matter where you travel, time will fly. Many times, you'll feel that you've only scratched the surface of what the area has to offer. You may wake up to find you didn't do what you'd envisioned. This can lead to lots of disappointment. This will especially hold true if it was an expensive trip.

Creating a theme is the number one key to a wildly successful trip!

A trip theme is vital to getting the trip experience that you desire. Three things are usually a good starting point for creating a theme. For instance, consider a trip to Italy. It's a huge country with so many things to see and do. Now, consider the same trip with the theme of Art, Architecture, and Eating. You could create a theme around France, Food, and Fashion. Even a stay-cation or a fun girls getaway can have a theme of Spa, Shop, Sleep, Repeat!

A theme can be very general in nature or very specific.

> *Author's Note*
>
> *On a solo trip to England, I went with the theme of history and mystery. I also like to keep track of the many forms of transportation taken during a trip. You could create a theme around a favorite food or drink. While in Italy, my daughter decided to have tiramisu at every restaurant. Each dessert presentation was completely different. What's a passion of yours? Gardening, a craft like knitting or sewing, tea or wine, libraries, the list is endless. When you create a theme you make the trip uniquely you!*

You could choose a favorite place to visit. One friend notes that she always checks out the local grocery store. She finds something and brings it home as a souvenir of her trip. In other words, your theme can be for one trip or for every trip. You can have multiple themes within a theme.

What's your passion? Art, beer or wine, books, cooking, gardening, music, shoes...the list is endless! I tend to search out botanical gardens, local markets, architecture, and history. I also like to find places where I can explore on foot.

Pick a word or words to provide the frame for your travel plans. You can create a theme for a trip or for the year. A national park theme could have you visiting all the parks near you or in your country. You could create a beach or mountain theme. How about an off-the-beaten-path theme?

Creating a theme will ensure you do the top things on your list. A theme helps you to not become distracted by shiny things that have nothing to do with your trip's goals. A theme does not mean you are becoming inflexible or won't allow moments of serendipity. Times when you go "off-script" may become the highlight of your trip. Yet, having a theme provides you with the sense you achieved what you wanted. Once you're home reliving your trip, you'll look back in contentment instead of frustration.

Now that you'd decided on your theme, it's time to consider how much money you'll need for your adventure.

Determining the Cost

For many, the idea of a dream trip brings up all the expenses involved. Often, the refrain is that "I can't afford to go anywhere. I just don't have the money."

Money isn't the issue.

Let me repeat that.

Money isn't the issue. It's the outlook.

But before I get into this topic, I want to talk about the difference between cheap and frugal. I like nice things. Who doesn't? However, my idea of a splurge may be different from yours. You alone can decide what your comfort level is when it comes to cost, convenience or comfort.

There are always ways to save money on your trip. At the same time, you need to feel okay with a bit of splurging on activities or things that you want.

Save Versus Splurge

I enjoy nice things. I just don't want to spend a lot of money to get them. Now if you already travel first class all the way, then I'm thrilled you're even reading this! However, you could be reading this because you may already travel well, but you want to travel more.

Or maybe you just want to travel more… or at all! Once you learn some travel hacks, you'll be on your way to packing your bag and jetting off to your next adventure. I believe there are ways to splurge while saving money and I think that you should splurge! What you desire that splurge to be is up to you. Your splurge may be totally different than another woman's idea of a splurge. No matter! That bit of splurging may end up as a wonderful memory or souvenir of your trip.

Once you decide where you want to go, that's when it's time to figure out how to travel well for less. When you've determined where you want to go and your theme, you can explore the options. Those options will provide insight into areas where you can save money.

For instance, traveling with others can often save you money. If you decide to take a tour, you may find you are charged a higher rate for a single. This is because the tour group makes their income from a certain number of travelers.

The first consideration is to decide where you want to save and where you wish to splurge. Are you okay with traveling in economy or would you prefer a higher travel class? Do you want to stay in a five-star resort or will a basic three-star hotel fulfill your needs and comfort level?

Transportation is one of the most significant expenses of almost any trip. The areas where you can save quite a bit involve food, drink, and activities.

Accommodations or lodging usually come in second to transportation in cost.

So, what should you focus on first?

You might have a preferred destination in mind, so you look at places to stay first. Conversely, you might find a great deal on a flight, so you grab that first.

Normally it may benefit you to:

- Pick the destination
- Investigate lodging for convenience, comfort and to get an idea of cost.
- Find airfare and book it.
- Secure lodging.
- Research activities and transportation at location.

There are lots of variables of which area should come first. However, for planned trips, gauging the cost of getting somewhere coupled with how much it will cost you for lodging once you arrive are two primary factors to consider.

Make a list of all the things that you will need for your trip. These may include:

Pre-trip costs (if any)

Transportation

Lodging or accommodations

Food and drink

Activity costs

Miscellaneous expenses

Post-trip charges (if any)

Pre-trip costs are those you will incur before your trip. These may include trip insurance, passport or visa fees, baggage, clothing, etc.) It could also cover any animal or child care expenses.

Transportation costs can be a significant part of your travel budget. How you get to your destination can add up quickly if you aren't careful. If you're traveling far, many individuals chose to fly. Airfare costs are where you can save quite a bit of money if you understand some simple flight hacks. It is also an area where you may want to save money on one part of your trip and splurge on another piece. There are many ways to travel--bus, subway, boat, bike, or scooter. Take more than one and enjoy the ride.

Lodging is another area where you can spend more than you need, or even should. The shorter your stay is when you can choose something fundamental or pick that as a time to splurge a bit. The longer your visit is when you want to spend less money while getting the form of lodging you prefer.

Food and drink expenses can add up. Always find a place that includes breakfast in the cost. That will save you the cost of a meal a day. That's why I highly recommend bed and breakfasts. On a trip to the Netherlands, our hostess provided us with fresh pastries, fruit, and cheese. She also had other items for cooking. We were able to eat breakfast and pack snacks for the day with what she provided for our morning meal.

Activities can also add a lot of expense to your trip. One of the easiest ways to save money is to buy a city pass. Combine transportation and activities, and you can save money along with time and frustration. In every city, you will find things that you can do that are free or cost you little. Some of your best memories may not be any of the standard tourist items on your checklist. Instead you'll recall a simple walk on a cobbled road. The enjoyable moment listening to music outside your room overlooking a piazza. That time you sought shelter from a storm in an establishment dating back to the early hundreds. Every city in every country has opportunities to enjoy activities for minimal or no cost. Research them before you go.

Miscellaneous Expenses is the area where planning can go awry. These expenses are what you might consider your "whoops" fund. Some costs you can expect such as trip souvenirs. Others are those things you don't plan like buying a new pair of glasses because yours broke. Or the trip to the clothing store because your luggage got lost. Or the visit to the emergency room because you didn't dismount the Segway properly. Things happen, and they happen no matter how well you plan. Therefore, travel insurance that also covers medical expenses or losses should be on your pre-trip expense list.

Plan for how much you'll allocate for daily purchases and a percentage for any mishaps.

Post-trip Expenses can also sneak up on you. Pay for as much of the trip up front, ahead of time. This includes activities, transportation, lodging, etc. You don't want to fall off your chair when you open your credit card bill the following month. And speaking of credit, only use it to get points and miles and pay off immediately. Use designated cards for minimizing or eliminating foreign transaction fees. But don't use credit cards if you don't have the funds to pay them off already set aside.

Now that you know the seven parts of your trip, you're ready to plan your dream trip.

Do Your Research

Planning is—or can be—as much fun as the actual journey. Really, it is. Planning is an extension of the trip. It builds up the anticipation and allows for great rewards. Of course, you can employ a travel agent or assign others to do the work for you. Just be fully cognizant that they make their living by earning commissions on what they sell to you. Or that others planning a trip are going to pursue their interests first. Neither is a bad thing. It's just a simple fact.

Researching your trip provides you with excellent insights and allows you to discover ways to save money. Stacking functions is a great way to decrease spending while increasing your trip's pleasure. For example, the Omnia card is a great card for Rome. This pass provided admittance to major attractions as well as a hop-on/hop-off bus. The pass allowed you to walk right into the attractions you want to see. Our group saved money on transportation costs to the different venues. Even better, the bus stopped a few blocks from where we were staying.

Airfare is another area where you can save money if you do research. Sometimes a round-trip ticket can end up costing you more. Flying out from a different location can save you money.

Generate a Budget

Yes, it's time to create the dreaded budget. Vacations can get out of hand if you don't figure out the costs upfront.

Create a budget range that allows some leeway in spending. This includes a top "splurge" amount as well as anticipated cost. It's fun to include a 'yippee' category for that great deal found in your research.

Consider making a range budget. For instance, let's say that you figure it will cost $3500 for your three-week trip. You might have a range of $2000 to $4500. Your budget might be $350 or $3500. The amount is just an example.

Always remember to consider comfort first, then convenience, then cost.

You can use a simple journal or a spreadsheet to create your budget for each area. This should include an overall projected budget. From there, create three columns on standard amount (anticipated amount you will spend), save (discounts and savings you've discovered in your research), and splurge (something you want to do if you're able to save enough in other areas).

Once you have your budget complete, you'll have a firm foundation of where you stand.

Prepare Your System

Creating a trip file is important because items can get lost in email threads, etc. There are myriad sources you can use for your system. There are also great trip applications that allow you to keep everything in one place in the cloud. Choose the system that works best for you whether a spreadsheet, a list, an app, etc. Creating a system is a vital step in keeping you on track and away from frustration.

Construct Your Itinerary

Being spontaneous is something I love. But I must admit that I'm a planner when it comes to creating trips. I like knowing I don't have to think about where I'm going to stay and that it's already paid for in full. I like identifying when a location is the least busy and more relaxed for the visit. So, a firm foundation of the basics works well for me. I know that no matter how much time you spend planning that the unexpected can and will happen. Therefore, it's important to leave in some downtime and not load up your days too much. Some of your best memories may be sipping a local wine, while eating olives and cheese on your veranda. Or wondering how you got on Parisian television because of a local strike.

Enjoy the Process!

Traveling is one of the most fulfilling things you can do in your life. It adds depth to your worldview. It introduces you to new countries, cultures, foods, and experiences. Travel makes each of us a better person.

A successful trip consists of five distinct parts:

- Planning
- Travel
- Destination
- Return
- Reflection

It's far more than the actual trip. The planning and the journey is as much fun as the real destination. The return to home and habit provides excellent insights into your personality. Reflection allows you to remember the trip with fondness.

There is no such thing as a perfect trip. But if you got to go and do what you wanted, then you have succeeded in having a wildly successful adventure. So, savor each piece to the fullest!

In the next chapter, you'll learn about lodging and the importance of picking the right accommodations for your trip.

Chapter Two

Lodging

Lodging usually come in second to transportation in cost. It's important to consider your comfort and safety level when deciding where to stay.

First, let's talk about safety and risk. There is no such thing as being risk-free. Where-ever you stay, common sense precautions are things that should be followed.

Larger establishments will often have safety protocols in place. Elevators may only go to individual floors after a designated hour. Protection may factor into the cost associated with staying at larger establishments. If staying in smaller facilities, carry your own rubber doorstops and detachable window alarms.

We'll start with most money out of pocket and least risk to least expensive and possible risk factors. Now there are caveats to both areas both in expense and in risk.

There are five primary types of accommodations available.

These are:

- *International Chain Hotels*
- *National Hotel Chains*
- *Boutique Hotels*
- *Bed and Breakfast Establishments*
- *Home or Apartment Rentals*

Staying in a large hotel may provide you with a feeling of comfort and safety. More people and staff do equate to a significant presence of people. Staying at a major hotel doesn't negate all safety concerns. Look for those that require key cards for elevators after a specific timeframe.

International Chain Hotels

Three ways to save money or gain benefits by staying in an international chain hotel. These are:

1. Get a Package Deal.
2. Score One or More Free Nights.
3. Figure in the Perks.

Buying through an aggregator puts the hotel and transportation under one cost. You may get a better deal though sometimes you can save money by purchasing separate items. The cost of the hotel may be included in the price of what it would normally cost you to fly to the destination. This isn't always the case though. Check first to see how much it would cost if you booked each area separately. Additionally, look at any package deals that offer an additional amount off their standard fares.

Many credit cards will provide you with intro reward points after you spend a certain amount. Credit cards that offer 40,000 to 100,000 bonus points after spending a certain amount offer you one to two free nights. Then it's your choice of where you want to spend that night. Many international hotel chains have multiple brands in myriad countries. Like airlines, it pays to have a membership with at least one major global chain.

Maybe you don't want to get a credit card, or you already have one. You can get a free night if you use some online sources and spend a specific night at hotels through them.

There are many ways to get rooms at minimal or no cost through focusing on credit card points. This book does not go into travel hacking. However, there are many books and sites devoted to learning how to maximize miles and points.

You may cringe at the thought of a standard hotel room charge, but if it includes some perks, it could be worth it. Do you like to sleep late? A later check-out is a benefit. Need a good meal before you head out for sightseeing? Find a hotel that includes a full breakfast. Major hotels may cater to weekly business travelers with free hors-d'oeuvres and drinks. Larger hotels will often charge a fee for in-room Wi-Fi. Find one that doesn't access a fee or get an upgrade, so Wi-Fi is free. Resort fees, parking, etc. can add up quick. You might find the additional perks will pay for the higher room rate.

Many international or large chains may be located close to sites you want to visit. A centralized location can decrease other associated costs such as transportation. If transportation to activities is as much or more than your lodging, it's not a bargain. Plus, you must figure in the time you're spending on travel. You'll want to maximize the time doing what you wish, not spending it in transport.

National or Regional Hotels

You may score better pricing or accommodations through remembering to:

1. Find out the business rates.
2. Book direct with the hotel.
3. Check-in at the "sweet-spot."

While some hotel chains associate with an international brand, that isn't always the case. A national or regional hotel may only have one establishment. Yet, it may have a global outreach. One way to save on costs is to drive to a local or regional spot. Having a staycation allows a break in routine. You can indulge in pampering without the added expense of airfare or other transportation.

You may find a cheaper weekly rate and a higher weekend rate at hotels that cater to businesses. Be open to changing hotels on the weekend, and you may save money by switching places. Conversely, if you plan on staying for at least a week, it may be better to stay in one place. Check out the hotel's weekly rates.

Consider comfort and convenience in relation to cost. An aggregator may offer a better price, but you'll have more chances of upgrades if you buy direct because the hotel must wait to receive payment through the aggregator. When you book direct and pay on arrival, hotels immediately collect the money. It may not happen in every case, but you may receive better rooms and service when booking directly through the hotel.

The way to extend your vacation or travel is to arrive early and leave as late as possible because this extends time at your destination. But that doesn't mean you need to check-in at that point. Ask to stash your luggage and head out to eat or do some exploring. Most of the time you will find that hotels have a check-out time of around eleven in the morning. Late checkouts can be around two in the afternoon. Housekeeping will clean the rooms during this time which is why most check-in's start at around three in the afternoon. Try to check in about 4:45 to 6:00 p.m. for the best opportunity to score a better room. Too early and you'll get the first open room which may not be in a great location. Too late and you'll get what's left after others have checked in to their rooms.

Additionally, ask for a discount of the regular room rate for checking in after ten in the evening. You can shave off quite a bit off the room price by asking for this discount.

Boutique Hotel

Boutique hotels have independent ownership and will often have less than 100 rooms. Boutique hotels offer some amenities that you may not find in traditional hotels. For instance, you may be able to bring your pet with you which could save on pet care costs. Since you're staying in a local establishment, you may find your hotel in the heart of the city.

For example, the boutique hotel, Paris Hotel Excelsior Latin is an excellent spot to start your sightseeing. You can take the RER train from the airport to the Luxembourg stop. From there it's an easy walk to the hotel. Another boutique hotel in that same area is the Hôtel Saint-Jacques. It is just down the street from the Pantheon. The Boulevard Saint Michel is the main cross-street and is a good place for shops, restaurants, and many sites.

Remember that while cost is a factor, convenience is also important. From Saint Michel, you can stroll to the Luxembourg gardens. The Pantheon and other attractions are less than a five-minute walk. Notre Dame Cathedral is about a fifteen-minute walk. An excellent location makes sightseeing convenient and saves on transportation. A boutique hotel is often recognized for its personality. Two such places in Colorado are the Brown Palace in Denver and The Stanley in Estes Park. The Brown Palace is full of history and serves tea in the lobby. The Stanley is where Stephen King got his idea for The Shining. Both hotels offer tours. If you enjoy a hotel while traveling but want something a bit more unique, then check into boutique hotels.

Just like major hotels, there are ways to save when staying at a boutique hotel. The following ideas can be applied to almost any lodging.

1. Staying Off-Season.
2. Don't forget your discounts.
3. Ask for an upgrade.

Off-season or shoulder season rates can significantly decrease your lodging expense. Bonus—not only will you get a less expensive room you'll often save in airfare and other costs. Be cognizant that shoulder season travel has pros and cons.

Pros:
- Less travel cost
- Lodging discounts
- Cooler temperatures (or sometimes warmer temps)
- Fewer crowds

Cons:

- Shops or main establishments closed or limited hours of operation
- Closures of family-run establishments
- Rainy or snowy weather

When traveling during the off-season, hoteliers are more apt to provide discounts to get you into their establishment.

Most hotels accept discounts. Discounts are available for students, military, over 55, membership groups or credit card holders. Don't leave money behind by not asking about any available discounts.

What if you have already gotten a discount? Is there anything else you could do to have a great experience? Yes, and it's as simple as asking what benefits are included in the room.

Sometimes we don't get what we want because we simply don't ask. Upper floors usually mean less noise as well as nicer views. Go check out the room provided. If you're not happy, go back, be polite and ask for a different room on a higher floor.

If you like hotels but really prefer interacting with others, bed and breakfasts are a great option. Especially when traveling solo, it's nice to connect with other travelers over a morning cup of coffee or an evening glass of wine. Some establishments may also offer dinner at an additional cost to the room. These dinners are well-worth doing as you can meet some of the most interesting people over dinner.

It is therefore not surprising that the bed and breakfast establishment is a favorite of this author.

Bed and Breakfast Establishments

Bed and breakfasts will often fall into three categories.

Formal Bed and Breakfast: The house is for guests only. It is spacious enough for many guests depending on the size and how many floors. Adam's Inn in Washington, D.C. falls into this category. Adam's consists of two houses that offer rooms. Like most formal bed and breakfasts, they include communal living and dining areas. Some offer kitchens, laundry, and office. Breakfast is in the dining room, and guests come and go during the breakfast hours. Guests have their own room or suite. Bathrooms are either en-suite or shared.

Proprietor Bed and Breakfast: The difference between a formal bed and breakfast and a proprietor bed and breakfast is that the owner lives on site. They may have a suite of rooms in the house or live in a cottage on the grounds. This type of bed and breakfast is smaller and may offer a few rooms or more. Unless the house is a castle, mansion or villa, most will feature less than ten guest rooms. Breakfast is served at a specific time versus a more extended timeframe found in a formal BNB. All guests eat at the same table. North Lodge on Oakland in Ashville, N.C. is one such bed and breakfast. Because there are fewer guests, you often receive a higher amount of personal help and service.

Family Bed and Breakfast: A family bed and breakfast is where the owner or family lives in the bed and breakfast. In a family establishment, you'll find one to two rooms or a suite of rooms that the family rents out for stays. These types of establishments work well for singles, couples, or small families.

Each has its own unique charms. Here's a quick overview on the differences on a monetary level.

A formal bed and breakfast can run as much if not more than a hotel. Yet, they may also provide perks that you desire. They may have an adults-only policy. They may have an afternoon happy hour. With a family bed and breakfast, you may get to know the family, and it could lead to a dinner invitation. For solo travelers, a bed and breakfast allow you a way to meet people and feel connected.

Ways to save with Bed and Breakfast Establishments:

1. Consider non-award winners.
2. Contact by phone or email.
3. Pay in advance.

When a bed and breakfast wins a lot of awards or is high on a travel advisory site, it almost guarantees rates are going to be higher and upgrades harder to score, though not always. There are many bed and breakfast's starting out that will be as nice as the winners or even more so. Plus, you'll be helping them to gain good reviews, so they may try harder with niceties in your room or for your use.

Call and inquire about the rates for the establishment. Talking with a person may get you a discount or an upgrade. Staying over a certain number of days may supply you with a discount or a free night.

Paying in advance may or may not get you a discount. It never hurts to ask if there is any discount for paying upfront. Some may not discount the cost, but you may receive an extra night at no charge.

Apartment or Home Rentals

I love the story of how a couple of broke college students decided to throw down a blow-up mattress and rent it. They kept building on their success and turned it into a billion-dollar industry. Today you'll find Airbnb, HomeAway, VRBO, and many others. These accommodations can vary. After bed and breakfasts, this is one of the best ways to travel in a group.

1. Live out a fantasy.
2. Stay off the beaten path.
3. Share the cost.

Years ago, an advertisement spoke of "living" where you're staying. Yes, you can still look out your hotel window and enjoy seeing the Nile glittering in the dark. But it's quite a different feeling of unlocking "your" front door. A home away from home allows you to grab a glass of wine and sit on your veranda overlooking the Mediterranean. Want a glimpse of how it would be to live where you're visiting? A rental often takes you away from the tourist traps and places you in a neighborhood

The farther you are from attractions, the less expensive you may find your accommodations. If you can access a bus or metro, or you have a vehicle, you can discover other treats of the area. Talking to your neighbors can give you insights into great local restaurants and little-known spots that only locals know. Serendipitous side trips make a trip special. Historic buildings and churches as well as art on the streets can all make for a great day out and cost nothing or a small donation. Remember the more free activities, the more money to find that perfect place to lay your head.

Traveling solo and as a group, both have their benefits. One significant advantage of going in a group is splitting the cost. You can do this in a hotel but share an apartment, and you're bound to have your own bed. Having a kitchen can save you money when you head down to the local grocer instead of eating out all the time. Depending on your location, if you rent a vehicle, the cost can be insignificant when divided between your group.

Other Lodging

Finally, you can stay at a motel or a cabin, a hostel, couch-surf, house-sit or sleep on the plane or train. Each of these has benefits for your budget. In some cases, they may have more risk involved. For some, the main risk is taking you out of your comfort zone. But these options can save you enough money to make that trip of your dreams.

What if you don't want to spend any money on accommodations?

Couch-surfing will save you money on hotels. Now there are different forms of couch-surfing. One way is that you sleep on the couch in a home with someone you don't know. In most cases, you'll find it isn't a literal couch but a spare bed. As more women are traveling solo, you can often find places that cater exclusively to women.

Up for adventure? Start putting the word out where you want to go. You may find a friend knows someone where you are traveling. It can also be the case of someone who knows someone who knows someone else. What a beautiful gift of hospitality for someone to allow you to stay in their home. While most people don't want any money for your visit, it's always thoughtful to provide some cash and goodies when you leave as a thank you. So, don't knock "couch-surfing" as you might meet some wonderful people.

House-sitting is growing in popularity and a great way to explore an area. You can find house sits for a few days to weeks to months. While you won't pay to stay there, this is one case where you have obligations. You are responsible for caring for the home in the owner's absence, and they may have pets or gardens. Housesitting is a great way to visit an area. There are many house-sits available across the globe. It's a great way to travel without spending a penny on accommodations.

If you're up for a bit of work while you travel, you can check out room exchange opportunities. Love manual labor around farming or gardening? Check out World Wide Opportunities on Organic Farms (WWOOF) or Help Exchange (HelpX). In many cases you can find work around the globe that fits your skillset or desire.

Sleeping on the plane or train is probably one of the least favorite things to do. Yet if it can save you a night of accommodation costs, it can sometimes be worth it.

In many travels away from your country, you are going to find yourself sleeping on the plane. Sleeping 'while' you travel is the time to consider comfort and cost. Spend the most money on the evening or overnight legs where you'll receive your dinner and try to sleep. How much is your hotel budget? Include that amount to your airfare cost to ensure a better flight experience and rest. Fly at night, and you will save money and get a better sleep experience if you upgrade. This can also be true for trains which is much nicer if you get a sleeper car.

Lodging is one of the most critical pieces of your trip. The place you stay is where you will begin your days and end your nights. Determine how to save money but don't scrimp on lodging. Where you lay your head, every night is one area where you need to consider comfort ahead of cost. When you can achieve both, you've won!

Chapter Three

Transportation

How you travel is as important, if not more so, than the actual destination. The travel portion can either add to the trip or detract from your experience.

The way you travel can impact your physical, emotional and mental health. In most cases (and for this book) there are five primary ways to get to your destination. They are:

1. Airplane
2. Automobile
3. Ship or boat
4. Train
5. Bus

Airplane

Comfort. Convenience. Cost. If you always look at flights with this in mind, you will find that you can often travel better for less money.

In the best scenario, this is the exact order of how you will enjoy air travel the most. However, to travel more, the less cost out of pocket the better. So how can you get the best seat while sticking to your budget?

Comfort

First, let's talk comfort.

How tall are you? How wide are you? These two areas make a significant impact on the comfort of the seat you choose. Do you have any body or health issues that could impact your comfort while sitting? Uncomfortable seat choice can be exacerbated by leg length, weight, health or other issues.

The fact is that the higher class (i.e., more expensive) of the seat, the more padding you will have. Thus, it's a good practice to carry a scarf, sweater, or inflatable pillow to pad your seat cushion.

Additionally, a higher class of seat will be broader. It may have a more profound recline or a footrest. A wider seat is vital for long flights as you will want to reposition yourself as much as possible. Your movement will be more constricted in smaller space parameters.

Key Considerations

Flight Length:

First, you need to look at the length of the flight. Next, determine your personal tolerance for a more confined space.

> **Two hours or less** can be okay for most people if no health issues are involved. In those cases, flying economy may be an economical choice.
>
> **Two to five hours** you'll want to get up, move around and stretch. If you are in a middle or window seat, getting up and down may be problematic. The longer the flight is when you want to consider an aisle seat or to upgrade to a premium seat with more legroom.

Five hours or more, try to upgrade to a better class for more comfort. Walk around. Do stretches. Research how to get a better class for the same or less money than economy.

Try not to take any flight that is over eight to ten hours in one leg if possible. Stretch, walk and wear compression socks. Spend more on this leg to ensure your health and wellness.

Seat Choice:

Airlines provide a standard economy service where you don't get to choose your seat. If you can select your seat, airlines are now charging ten dollars, twenty dollars or even more.

Again, this is a personal preference and relates to comfort as well as convenience.

Window seats are great if you like to look outside or get a bit claustrophobic. They are also good to prop a pillow against if you are traveling in economy. You can face the window wall when sleeping. Conversely, you will have to ask two other people to move when needing to use the bathroom or get up to walk around. Your position isn't as much of an issue when everyone is awake but not so great for all involved when people are trying to sleep.

Window seats on smaller aircraft will also have less space due to the outer shell configuration. This can mean that you may have less room on the side next to the window.

Whenever you choose your seat check to see if there are any obstructions in the foot area. Sometimes there will be boxes that negate being able to fully stretch out your legs.

The aisle seat is a better selection if you tend to get up and walk about quite a bit. It's also better if you need to visit the restroom more often or have a tight connection to another flight. You must keep arms and legs from getting run over by trolleys or tripping people heading to the restroom. This is also where many a poor traveler in the aisle seat get hit on the head by people removing luggage from overhead bins. For overnight flights, being on an aisle may prove more disruptive to sleep.

Finally, there's the middle seat. Avoid if possible unless you are traveling with a companion. If you are traveling with others, it may make sense to consider purchasing the middle seat if traveling as a couple or with family or friends. You can raise the seat rests in the middle and have that additional space to stretch out. But you may find that you could have gotten a better class seat with more amenities for the same price. Price variation is why you should check all the fees before making your decision.

Don't assume that an economy seat is always going to be less costly than an upgraded seat. Review all the costs before making a decision. You may find that upgraded seat costs one hundred dollars more. However, when you add in the cost of purchasing your seat, the cost of any checked bag and having to purchase a meal, the upgraded seat may come out as equal or less in cost.

Seat Placement:

You can choose a bad seat in any class. For instance, if you are over 5'4", don't get a seat next to a bulkhead. It's great for space in front of you for shorter trips. However, it has a drawback for taller people as you will be unable to fully stretch out your legs. Because of it, you will have bent limbs, the entire time of the flight. Thus, if you are taller, select a seat where you can stretch your legs out under the seat in front of you.

Additionally, if there is a wall behind your seat, you won't be able to recline. No recline on an over-night or long flight makes for a very uncomfortable trip.

To find out the best seat choices and placement, you can check out Seat Guru. They mark the best seat choices in green and seats with issues in red. Don't choose seats close to galleys and restrooms where activity or noise prevents sleep.

Convenience:

Your choice of seat will also carry over into convenience. If you are in first or business class, you will be able to board first. If it's a short flight, you may want to board later. Use this extra time out of the plane in a lounge or to get in a bit of standing or walking. You will also be able to exit faster.

As you book your flights, think in terms of convenience. If you are catching another flight with a tight connection, being seated in the front of the plane can make a big difference for you catching a flight.

With an upgraded ticket, you'll receive snacks and complimentary beverages. In some cases, if your travel is during a meal time, you will also receive a meal.

Food served won't make up for additional cost incurred but can be helpful if you were unable to eat before boarding.

Upgrades also come with perks. Often, you'll receive pre-check for TSA with a seat in business or first class if you do not already have it. It's nice not having to put on a show for a guy in the photo booth or to have to remove your jacket or shoes.

A higher class will often supply you with one to two checked bags at no cost. You can save hundreds of dollars if you plan to check bags. It's also a good perk if you intend to bring back a box with a must-have souvenir of your trip.

Finally, when selecting your seat, you'll want to consider cost.

Your perfect airline seat is comfortable, convenient and provides contentment about the cost of your ticket.

Cost

Whether you find a great deal or use miles to book your flights, cost is a factor for most of us. But don't be fooled into thinking you can't fly in a better class for the same or even less money.

As much as possible, utilize travel hacking principles through credit cards to receive free flights. The only thing that would be better than getting a business class ticket to Paris from Denver for five dollars would be getting the first-class ticket for the same price.

Every day the costs you incur through what you purchase are ways to earn miles for flights and points for free hotel stays. This book does not go into the in's and outs of travel hacking but it is an area you'll want to learn if you want to travel more and travel well.

Let's say that you are traveling, and you will be bringing one carry-on and one checked bag. Although it's best if you pack light, sometimes checking a bag may make sense. Indeed, if you are flying home, checking a bag means one less thing to haul around. If your bag does get lost in transport, you will have other clothing and your luggage will be delivered to you at home.

You've also seen that you will be connecting around lunch. You also note a few hours between connections. During that time, you anticipate that you'll grab a bite at an airport restaurant.

Let's look at a real scenario.

Chicago to London.

The first place you might start to check costs is Google Flights to get a price range for seats.

As of this writing, Google gives us a range of $600 (round trip/RT) to $1200 (RT) for a seat in economy.

Start by creating a budget range with three categories.

First, the amount you expect to pay. In this case, let's say $800. Then jot down a figure that you would be happy if you could pay it instead—so that might be $600. Finally, if you could get an upgraded seat, how much would you be willing to spend? For this example, we can say $1000. So, your budget range is $600 to $1000.

Once you have the range you want to pay, you're now ready to start searching for the perfect seat.

There are many good airline flight searches. Pick a couple, so you get a good idea of flights and seat choices.

In this example, the following airlines were found for this route: Wow, Porter/Norwegian, and WestJet.

Wow has a no-frills approach which gives a cost of $380 (RT) with its premium class at $606 (RT). Norwegian would be $659 (RT) for economy or $1418 for premier level. Note that many smaller airlines only offer a club or premier class which is like a business class. However, if I go to the direct site for Norwegian, I can effectively cut my costs to fly with them in half or even less.

Researching further, we find $813 for economy and $2265 for premier economy on American or British Airways. British Airways has a high tax on their flights, so you might be able to book through miles but may end up paying much more in taxes and fees.

As you can see, there's a substantial cost difference between regional and larger airlines. Yet, if you have benefits or can gain miles, you may choose to spend a bit more.

So how can you save money and get the best seat?

- Be flexible on your dates.
- Search during the week.
- Search about 100 days out for international flights and about 50 days for domestic flights.
- Fly on Tuesdays, Wednesdays, Saturdays or on actual holidays.
- Fly early or late.
- Use miles wisely.
- Be willing to do your research by checking various search engine sites.
- Understand the taxes and fees for the airlines you want to fly.

Before planning any trip, if possible be flexible with the dates you leave and return. It could save you quite a bit in cost while providing you a much nicer travel experience. The difference in leaving a day earlier or later can be the difference of hundreds of dollars or lots of additional miles.

Any time you travel off season will save you in transportation costs. The best days to travel are mid-week, usually on a Tuesday or Wednesday or a Saturday. Time of day can also impact costs.

But there are always ways to find deals throughout the year. This book is not intended for those wanting to find the cheapest deal. This book is about helping you spend the least for the best experience.

First, secure miles through a credit card. At this writing, you can fly domestically on a round-trip ticket for 25,000 miles. In most cases, current miles will set you back around 30,000 miles one way in economy for an international flight from the United States to Europe. A business class ticket is approximately 60,000 miles and a first-class ticket in the range of 100,000 miles. These will vary depending on airline, but this is a general approximation of miles required for each type of service.

Because you want to use your miles the best way possible, don't use them on short legs or even for domestic flights unless it works in with your plan. Save your miles for the main leg of the trip where you'll want more comfort for sleeping.

The first important thing is to determine how to best use the miles you have. Always check the cost from your home airport to your destination. Then check the cost from your primary launch airport to your destination.

Finally investigate the costs of flying out of or into a different airport. Keep track of the various costs and factor any costs of transportation to that destination.

If you tend to fly with one airline, note their hubs and fly out of those hubs for better pricing and connections.

Let's say that you have a budget of $800 for a roundtrip flight to Europe. You also have 100,000 in miles.

Pick the airline that flies out of your home hub. From that you're also going to want to know their alliance network. Once you have that information, you can begin your research.

First, look at the cost from your home airport to your destination. Open the ones that suit your budget and schedule. On those, look to see where they connect if the flight is not non-stop. In many cases, flying out with a 'positioning' flight can save you a lot of money. Write down the cost for economy, premium economy, business and first. This gives you a gauge of various costs and benefits associated with each seat.

After you've looked at the cost of the flight, close it out and open another search but click 'redeem miles.' You want to know how much it will cost in miles to fly the same route.

The first thing you will want to do is go to your airline's mileage calendar. It will show you an economy area and a business/first area.

Open the full calendar and see the best days for lower mileage amounts.

You may note that the awards may vary from day to day. For a business or first-class ticket, one day could show

50,000 in miles, the next day 60,000 and the following day 90,000.

On your first research pass, look at a round-trip ticket. On the next pass, investigate a one-way ticket. Sometimes the cost can be better as two one-way tickets instead of a standard round-trip ticket.

You may also want to fly into one airport or country and fly out of a different airport or country depending on your itinerary.

If you don't have enough miles for a flight, you can still get some good deals by flying regional airlines or airlines needing to fill flights.

Now how would you determine what's the perfect seat for you?

- Determine your preferred comfort level.
- Resolve the issue of convenience.
- Establish the cost you want to pay.

These three areas are useful for any travel expenditures whether airfare or choosing lodging.

Travel should be about the most comfort for the less cost. Therefore, it's important to take your time and do research thoroughly.

Now let's move into the other forms of transportation.

First, let's look at vehicle transportation. Traveling by vehicle includes shuttles from airports, taxis, tuk-tuks, etc. For this section we are going to focus on automobile rentals.

Automobile

If you will not be in a place where public transportation is accessible, or you are needing to convey a group, then you may choose to fly somewhere and rent a vehicle to travel around your destination.

If you reserve a vehicle at the airport, it's often convenient and depending on the time frame of your travels, may be an acceptable cost. However, taking a short bus or metro ride to an off-site location may save you hundreds of dollars as you do not have to pay the airport charge incurred by the rental company that is passed on to you. Some rental firms have shuttles taking you away from the airport for this reason.

Reserve in advance. You can get a better daily fee and may be able to gain a better vehicle or upgrade. As with airlines or hotels, having a membership with a rental company may afford you some benefits.

Rental companies will often encourage you to purchase their insurance. In the United States of America, vehicle insurance covers the person. So, renting a car will also include your personal automobile insurance. But only to a point. In places like the United Kingdom, the insurance covers the vehicle, not the person. Therefore, it's important to understand the difference in whatever location you are traveling. Know exactly what is included and how it may affect you should you find that an accident has occurred.

Many times, people will rent through a credit card that provides vehicle rental insurance. However, this is a time to read that fine print! It may be that coverage only kicks in after other insurance claims are settled. Or it could be that the insurance coverage is for a much smaller amount with a more substantial deductible.

Here's one story. An accident occurred. The woman spent months trying to resolve the issue. She had to go back and forth between the rental car company, her insurance and credit card company. She'd chosen not to purchase the vehicle rental company's insurance, believing she had coverage. If she had taken the rental coverage, she would have simply dropped off the keys and left. Again, we are brought back to the importance of considering convenience and cost. In many, if not most cases, you may not have any issue, but it's that one time that can cause havoc in your vacation plans.

Ship or Boat

Cruising has gained in popularity over the years. It combines lodging, transportation, meals, and activities all in one fee. Like every other form of transportation, traveling by boat has its pros and cons.

Some people love cruises which can range from $600 per person on a large ship to $9000 for a smaller cruise line. Some ships stop at ports and are gone within a day allowing you to sample various countries. These ports are primarily along a country's coastline. Others may travel up a riverway.

Cruises are useful for those who don't want to unpack at each destination. Cruising is also a better fit for those content with exploring coastal and sometimes, more touristy areas. The downside is you only get to see a small glimpse of various countries. There is not as much time for exploration as you must return to the ship within a particular time frame. Tours may be part of the price which can save you money. You may also find yourself in a large group versus being able to explore on your own.

Smaller ships often travel inland and have fewer passengers. These ships, commonly called longboats, also stop at ports of call. A more modest ship may provide a more leisurely experience. Other ships that may fall into this category are large sailboats, clippers, etc. These boats may also be more expensive but will often offer deals.

Another way to travel by boat and save some of the costs is to take a repositioning cruise. A repositioning cruise is when a ship moves from sailing in one region to another region. Repositioning cruises occur when ships move to other ports as the season's change. Repositioning cruises offer specials and perks as you will be spending more time at sea. Thus, repositioning cruises provides a lot of sea days for relaxing. If you enjoy a more leisurely approach to travel, then this may be something to explore.

What if you want to take your time traveling but you want to see more of the country? Then train travel may be your best choice.

Train

In many countries, travel by train is a great way to travel. For instance, the United Kingdom has an excellent train system. You can buy a rail pass for England or Europe if your plans are taking you to major cities. Traveling by train is an easy way to explore countries and see areas that you will miss if you take an airplane or a ship. The Eurostar connects London to Paris in a short two hours.

Just like airplanes or other forms of travel, there are different levels of service.

First class affords a nicer, wider seat. In this carriage, you often have a table or other amenities. Most importantly for many travelers, upper classes have plugs for your electronic devices. You will also receive some free snacks or meals when you purchase a first-class ticket. There is also a designated space for your luggage. Upper classes are often quieter.

In economy class, you will receive a basic smaller seat. While the first class will have two seats across, economy class will include three. Your luggage will need to be held in front of you if no overhead space is available. There are no charging devices at every seat. If snacks are served, you must buy them.

For overnight travel, you have the option of sleeping in your seat like on an airplane or purchasing a cabin. Remember that sleeping on a train will cut out one night at a hotel. By adding what you're willing to pay for a night in a hotel, you can often receive a more comfortable seat. By factoring in the conveniences and upgrades, you may still stay within your budget.

For a few hours or when you need to travel across the continent, buses are another option.

Bus

While travel by bus is not as popular in many areas of the world, it is still heavily used in others. In some larger cities, bus lines compliment a metro or subway system. However, a bus can take you to places beyond large towns that a plane may not be able to reach. In many cases buses are best used for shorter travels or those times when you want to see more of the country.

At this writing, Flixbus travels to around 1,400 destinations over twenty-six European countries. Buses often have multi-city passes for European cities. The cost for such passes can vary. If you're traveling on a tight budget, taking a bus provides you a great way to tour areas you desire to visit.

For your travels, you will use at least a couple of different forms of transportation. It's often fun to keep track of how many types of transport you use. Including forms of travel experienced could be another theme you add to your travel plans.

TRAVEL MORE. TRAVEL WELL. TRAVEL SOON.

Notes

Chapter Four

Activities

The activities you pick relate to what you enjoy as a person. If you travel with your family or a group, daily outings may include things that you don't enjoy as much.

As noted earlier, whether you are on a solo trip or traveling with others, one of the most important things you can do to have a successful trip is to create a theme. This theme could be the theme for the entire trip or it could be a daily theme. If you are traveling with others, ask them to share one or two words or thoughts about what they want for the trip. Then combine it all to create a theme that works for everyone.

It's especially important to have some plan concerning activities. Will you pick something that everyone does together, or will there be times that individuals go off exploring by themselves or in pairs? Are you willing to oversee a day if you are willing to take a backseat on another day? All these are important things to consider and talk through before you arrive at your destination.

Before the trip:

Once you have your main words—you can start doing your research into your trip. Research the area where you are traveling.

Events

Find out if any events are happening while you are there. Knowing what is on the calendar where you're heading is vital for two reasons. On the upside, you may be able to participate in something that you would enjoy. On the downside, there may be more people in the area and transportation may be harder to obtain. Costs may be higher during that time as well. If you're not aware of a marathon or parade or other street closure, what you thought might be a ten-minute commute can easily turn into hours of detours.

Weather

Check out the weather. The idea of sipping a refreshing drink while you lay on a beach chair may sound divine. Don't find yourself stuck with a far different reality of arriving during monsoon season. Being stuck in a hotel room fighting off mosquitoes will quickly dampen your enthusiasm. There's a saying that there is no bad weather, only bad clothing. While not totally true, having the right outerwear or footwear can make a big difference if the weather turns nasty.

Highlights

Decide on the highlights. Traveling to another place to visit for a specific period will dictate your focus. You won't want to return home and feel you didn't get to do what you thought would be the highlight of the trip. Make a list of the sites you want to visit and rank them in order of importance to you. If you're traveling with others, have them do the same thing. Also, remember that this doesn't have to include a specific site. Your highlight could be as simple as eating gelato while strolling the Ponte Vecchio. It could be taking in a view of some ancient ruins or a place of spiritual importance. You may enjoy walking in the garden or home of an author you've long admired. It could be that you want to try the local delicacy. As you can see the list is endless because it revolves around your desires. A highlight for you may be vastly different than a highlight for others.

Cost

Activities are what add to your trip. They can also add to the cost of the trip. Thus, it's critical you create a projected budget for your trip. Then you can look at the price and the desire to experience that activity. I prefer a combination of free events with those that cost money. But for those that do charge, you are going to want to save on cost as much as possible. So always check if there is a city pass offered. Passes will cut your expenses and often provide you some discounts. Talking with locals can give you some insight into free days or ways to get discounts for certain exhibits.

City Passes

Passes allow you entrance to a primary number of activities. These are often attractions such as museums, historic sites, etc. After that, it may also provide discounts for other attractions in the area. In most cases, you also have the option to use a hop-on, hop-off bus. Yes, they're "touristy." But the fact is that you are a tourist. So be willing to utilize some of the things that help you get more for less. Conversely, as much as possible, using these for primary areas will allow you to enjoy going off the beaten path for other activities.

Bus Passes

Check out both local public transportation buses and the tourist hop-on, hop-off buses. While they may be a bit not to your taste, they are great in helping you to recover from jetlag while still seeing the city. Using these buses help you gain your bearings of the city and hear some history or insights. The bus may go places you wouldn't have explored on your own. Bus passes will save time and your feet by taking you to the sites you want to visit. Even if you don't use a hop-on, hop-off tourist bus, many cities will have a good bus service that will allow you to see parts of the city you normally wouldn't and to provide an inexpensive way to get from Point A to Point B.

Itinerary

Once you've determined where you want to go and what you want to do, then map it out. If you have a certain amount of days to spend in one location, you will want to use that time wisely. Therefore, once you've mapped out the spots on the map, you can create an itinerary for the day. The best way to do this is by dividing the area up into quads. Then do one quad a day. You will see more and do more by following this method. Almost every place that you visit will be able to be marked up into quads. Not only will this provide you with an itinerary for the day, it will save you in transportation costs and time spent traveling between sites. By placing your activities in a quad, you can seek out other fun activities within the area as well as local eating establishments.

Packing

Where you are going and what you will do while there should be the basis for what you will bring regarding luggage. If you plan on dining out in high-end restaurants every evening, then stilettos may make sense. If you are out hiking every day and enjoying a nice hearty dinner, then skip the heels or cocktail dress. After you have your itinerary, you can then create a clothing list for each day.

In most cases, a shirt or blouse with a pair of slacks or a skirt will take you through every activity. Add in a scarf to dress up your outfit and for extra warmth and a jacket for colder or rainy days. Include a swimsuit, and you have a complete capsule wardrobe. A pair of cute ballet-style flats will work well for eating dinner or exploring ancient churches.

Walk

No matter where you travel—whether Florence's cobblestone roads or a local amusement park-you'll be walking—a lot. It's not uncommon to walk 15,000 to 20,000 steps daily and climb the equivalent of ten stories. If you're not a walker already, get out and start walking. Increase your steps and do another exercise as well like a stretching or balancing exercise like yoga or tai chi. Most importantly, make sure you have a great pair of shoes that are newer and work well. You don't want to break in shoes on your trip or find that the insole no longer supports your foot.

Boost your Immunity

The more you increase your immunity before the trip, the better. Building a healthy immune system will help you to fight off any germs or viruses that you contact while traveling or in your location. Get a good multi-vitamin and minerals into your system. Take an immune-boosting tincture or tonic daily. Address any current health issues that could cause a flair up on your travels.

On the Trip

Beating Jetlag

If possible arrive at the new location early in the morning with plenty of daylight ahead. While this isn't always possible, an earlier arrival may help with jetlag. First, you'll grab some sunlight which will help reset your internal clock. Avoiding jet lag is a good reason to drop your bags at your lodging and get out and explore. During this time try to get in a long walk. Even taking the metro will supply some exercise through climbing stairs and standing. The more you move, the easier it will be to avoid that first-day slump. However, should you feel your energy waning, it's not worth getting cranky. So, despite what you may have heard, if you are really feeling ill, take a quick nap. Quick being the keyword here. If you're not one who can do that, then avoid the nap. Maybe a nice shower or some other soothing or invigorating activity will help.

Who's in Charge

There are usually two types of people—those who like leaving all the details to others and those who like to be in charge. If you are traveling with others, each person will have their own agenda. Avoid hurt feelings and frustration by allowing one person to oversee the day. Even children can partake in this. There can still be an underlying agenda for the day (maybe around the specific sites), but the person in charge picks where to eat, what to enjoy and what to do. Anyone who has traveled with others knows that it's the little things that can cause problems. One person can get upset, or their feeling hurt if they feel that they have no say or control over the situation. When staying in different places, let each woman handle all the details for one area. Not only will it make individuals happy, but it will lighten the load, so no one must do all the planning.

Food

Yes, food is an activity! Of course, we have to eat to live. However, when you're traveling, it becomes part of the enjoyment of the trip. Take the time to have a nice leisurely meal every day. Spend that time getting to know your travel companions or yourself. Strike up a conversation with a couple sitting next to you. Some of your favorite memories may be around the various places that you enjoyed eating a meal. Conversely, food can also add to the cost. So, enjoy a plentiful breakfast one day with a simple lunch. Eat some toast and fruit for breakfast and indulge in a hearty dinner. In other words, break up the types of meals you eat. Eating good food can be one of the highlights of travel. Yet, over-indulge on fatty or other rich food, and you may find yourself stuck in your hotel room for a few days. Be cognizant of your digestion and how various foods make you feel.

Moving

As noted, the best thing that you can do for jetlag is move. But it is also good for the mind and body. It will provide a great way to see places that aren't on your list. So as much as possible, walk, then take the metro, train or bus around the city. Walking is an essential activity of your trip. It allows you to enjoy your destination at a slower pace while seeing more. Consider walking as window-shopping your destination. You'll be surprised what you find!

Serendipity

Don't over-schedule your days. Yes, you may think that you'll never return. That's even more reason to explore paths away from tourist destinations. Allowing for a bit of spontaneity may become the most memorable parts of your trip. Don't say you'll come back to something or you'll check it out "next time." Allow yourself the indulgence of doing or seeing something right then. See something that catches your eye, indulge your senses. Enjoy an artist playing music or painting a picture—stop and take an entire minute or more to appreciate their gift.

Activities should be a combination of those you're willing to pay for and those that are free.

Make a list of every activity and narrow the list down to your top ten. Focus on that group. It doesn't matter if the tourist areas or museums are at the bottom of your list. Make the trip one that makes you happy, not one that checks off an expected tourist list.

This is extremely important when it comes to museums. Yes, enjoy museums. But museums could be in any country in the world. If you have a short time at your destination, do you want to go inside a museum or do you want to enjoy the actual culture? That's a personal preference but the shorter the time you have at a destination, spend less time inside of museums that don't offer what you want to experience. This is not saying to avoid museums. They are treasures in each of their respective home cities. It's simply important to feel as if you've achieved what you wanted on the trip not what others may do or expect.

Chapter Five

Safety

Safety is an important part of every trip. There are areas within your power to assist with keeping you and your possessions safe while traveling.

Before the Trip

Purchase Travel Insurance

It is always wise to carry insurance for things that occur which are out of your control.

There are various types of travel insurance. Credit cards often provide the simplest of travel insurance surrounding trip delays or cancellations, lost luggage and may include rental car protection. However, this may be after your other vehicle insurance is used, so check the fine print!

Travel insurance is good for cases where you may have an unexpected reason you cannot make the trip. Maybe an accident, an illness or family emergency prevents you from your initial plans. Travel insurance can help cover associated costs incurred for the trip.

One of the most important reasons to purchase travel insurance is for medical emergencies. Comprehensive insurance policies will often include medical expenses and evacuation costs. Even if you have health insurance in your country, it may not cover ambulance, doctors or hospital costs in other countries. Stories abound of travelers who has experienced a medical emergency have been expected to pay thousands of dollars before they could leave the country. As this has happened to more than one traveler, it's safe to assume that it could happen to you also. If you need to be flown back to the country due to a serious medical condition, that can add up to the tens of thousands of dollars. Having travel insurance that covers medical expenses, travels to medical care both in the country and if required, back to your home country, is critical. In the worst case scenario, some companies provide burial expenses or transportation of remains back to your home.

You can look into various travel insurance companies and select the one that works with your needs and budget. You can also review the travel company through AM Best which rates travel insurance companies. By acquiring travel insurance for your needs, it will provide peace of mind should something happen to you while traveling.

Protect Credit Cards, Passport, Important Documents

Set up travel alerts on your phone for the cards you are planning to take. Only take cards that are necessary. Have a spare card that connects to your bank should your wallet or purse be stolen. Then you will still have a source to get cash while abroad. Besides setting up travel alerts, you will want to write down the numbers for your credit cards and contact information of your bank and credit card companies. Note that you don't want to take a picture in case your phone or computer is taken, damaged or not working. You can use this book to write down the credit card contact numbers but don't put all your information in this book where thieves could access it. If you plan on writing down private information where it could be possible for someone to access it, then create your own code on the information listed.

You will also want to get radio-frequency identification (RFID) sleeves. In today's world, thieves are looking for access to your cards and identity. Even with a wallet or bag fitted with RFID, this gives you extra protection when removing it from its pocket. In addition to credit cards, you can get them for your passport or other important documents.

Take a picture of your passport and have it on your phone. Print off a copy and put in your luggage. Email yourself (least protection) or create an online storage account where you store all your document information—passport, credit cards, travel insurance documents, visas (if required), etc.

Research your Destination.

If in the USA, check the State Department's website. Even if everything is clear, if you are traveling to an area where there is any unrest—pretty much all of the world currently—you can make your embassy aware of your presence in the country. The easiest way to do this is through the Smart Traveler Enrollment Program (STEP) for United States citizens. Canada also has a similar program, the Registration of Canadians Abroad. Australia's program is at smarttraveller.gov.au. If you are from another country, check to see if your state department has a similar service.

Find out any areas that you may not want to travel. Find out what train or metro stops attract the most pick-pockets.

Map out your area. Download or screenshot a map. Review a visual map to see where you will stay. Look at the opposite side of the street. "Visually" walk down a block in either direction. Pick out landmarks that will help guide you when you arrive. It's easy to get turned around in a new place. Having touchstones helps prevent problems.

There are various offline map apps that you can use. Check out these offline maps for use while traveling: MAPS.ME, Navmii World, HereWeGo, OsmAnd are a few to research. You can download others like Google Maps, Waze, etc. or take a screenshot.

Create a Plan

Email or leave an itinerary with your family. If you don't have a will, have that done. Provide your family with your wishes concerning burial or cremation if you die abroad. Chances are, nothing is ever going to happen. But you want to prepare for how you want things handled in that rare case. You also want to ensure that things are prepared for your family.

During Your Trip

Sadly, thieves are even on airplanes now. For carry-on bags, bring a TSA-approved lock and lock your bag. Conversely, even a carabiner can work to make your bag less attractive to thieves.

You may wish to wear a neck or waist pouch for your cards, important documents, and some cash. Having these items on your person is also good in case of having to evacuate a plane quickly and you're unable to take your purse. You can also place any valuables in various containers, put on the bottom of your bag and place other items like scarves, books, makeup kit, on top.

One of the least expensive but most effective items for travel safety is the simple carabiner. Attach a locking carabiner to your purse and luggage. On buses, metros, or trains, you can secure all your bags together. A thief may be able to grab one of your items but will have a hard time when you've attached them all together or hooked them onto a pole. Take a few different sizes. They are also great for use of hanging clothing to dry in the shower, securing items like cameras, and for hooking bags to chairs.

Leave none of your belongings in a rental vehicle. Even if your vehicle has an alarm system, many times the back windows on SUV's don't have alarms. It's easy for thieves to know this and pull suitcases or other valuables out the back windows without setting off the alarm.

If you get lost, go into a local store and ask for directions. Get insights before you travel on safe and unsafe areas. On metros when you hear announcements around securing your valuables, this is a signal pickpockets may focus on that area.

Most importantly don't plug your nose into your phone or get distracted taking pictures. Look up and be aware.

Don't make yourself a target. Solid colors in muted tones work well in most situations. Anything you wear that causes you to stand out will point you out as a potential target. Wearing comfortable shoes is important but they don't need to be bright white sneakers which scream "tourist." Keep jewelry simple when you're traveling. For instance, one or two rings, and some earrings. Use a scarf instead of a necklace. A leather band instead of a gold bracelet. When walking on the street, always secure your purse on the inside walk away from motorcycles or runners. A crossbody messenger bag is harder to steal than a large bag with a flimsy strap that can be cut.

Traveling with another person or a friend can help you stay safe sometimes. However, more women are enjoying independent, solo travel.

Traveling solo? Purchase a set of large frame sunglasses and attach a small mirror to them that are used by bikers. These small mirrors are especially useful for seeing who is behind you as you walk or when you have to stop to get money.

If possible, find a bank ATM that is indoors when withdrawing money. This may also prevent your card being skimmed by thieves who place readers over the ATM. In case you have to use an outdoor ATM, do so when it is light and if traveling with others, have another person turn around so that you are facing back to back.

Sightseeing areas and heavily touristed places are often where thieves congregate and wait for their chance to strike. In some areas, it's a fact that predators, and even guardians, force children into a life of crime. It's easy to trust children. They'll ask to take a picture with you and the next thing you know your bracelet or wallet is gone. Avoid areas where one person tries to sell you something (postcards, etc.) while another person takes your valuables.

Thieves often work in pairs or teams. Often a person will bump you so that you focus on them while another thief steals your purse, jewelry or goes through your pockets or bag. Be especially wary in crowds (on the metro, trains, etc.) where this can occur in mere seconds.

Also, avoid planned distractions. When everyone is distracted is when thieves can easily go after their preferred target. If you see a crowd gathered or looking toward a noise, that's when thieves can strike.

If a woman is traveling solo, she may gain unwanted attention or feel more threatened. Attackers may seek lone victims. Some ways to mitigate sharing your solo status is to wear a ring on your left hand as a way to deter unwanted advances or attention. If you feel someone has been following you or stalking you, change subway cars. Walk on the other side of the street and go into a store. Often you can merge into a group of people and appear to be part of the group you've joined.

In hotels or other lodging, many places are now cognizant of not giving out room numbers, or any information. Still you can always ask for two keys at hotels. This implies two people will share the room. If you are out by yourself, you can always become an actress and share with the waiter or bartender about your room-mate, spouse, friend, etc., meeting you later.

For extra lodging safety, carry a portable alarm device. This noise-making device attaches to a window or door. It's easy to stick a rubber stopper in your luggage which prevents doors from being opened. If you go out for the evening, leave a television or radio on so that your room appears to have someone inside. Stay at smaller bed and breakfasts where it's harder for those who don't belong to linger. Some hotels provide cards that take you to floors that are password-protected after a certain time of the evening.

In addition to watching what you eat or drink for health purposes, if you are traveling solo it is good to know of your surroundings so that no one can add anything to your drink while you're occupied in another direction.

Your demeanor has a lot to do with the way they perceive you. Act like you're a strong, no-nonsense savvy woman traveler. This is especially important if you are traveling solo. We're taught to be polite but when someone you don't know approaches you, they may be a friendly stranger or a potential threat. Trust your gut. If someone or someplace feels wrong, trust it. <u>Immediately.</u> Detach yourself from the person or leave the area without delay. It's easy to stop and question what we're feeling. In that time, someone can strike. It's better to feel that you may have been foolish than to be harmed. We women are bad about calling our feelings "silly." Our intuition is one of our greatest gifts as a woman. Use it.

Surprisingly, a simple whistle may be the main deterrent that helps stop someone from pursuing you. If you have sensed someone following you, you have moved across the street, and they are still approaching, then turn and face toward them and use the whistle. One of two things may occur. That person who is going about their business may think you've lost your mind, or the stalker will take off as now attention is on them.

Your life is more precious than anything you own. If a thief wants your wallet or jewelry, let them have it. If possible, throw it in the opposite direction and run away. It's best if your main money, papers and phone are kept away from your purse if possible. Then if a thief steals it, they won't get much of your money and nothing you can't replace.

Conversely, any threat to your person should be met with force. In that case, you will want to strike out in the most vulnerable areas—the eyes, slamming the heel of your hand under the nose, stamping the arch of the foot, jabbing your fingers into the neck.

To feel more confident while traveling, take a basic women's safety course. You can find these online that you can watch but you need to practice them. If you can take a class where you live, you may gain valuable insights into protecting yourself should the need arise. Taking these classes will also raise your confidence level. Statistics show that attackers and thieves often seek out victims who are not showing confidence or that look like they won't fight back.

> *Author's Note:*
>
> *Always listen to your gut and do what you feel is best, even if it seems out of the norm. I was once on a trip to the Middle East where my friend had a fanny pack she was using. Side note don't ever use something like that which are easy targets. In it, she had her nice camera she'd been using the entire trip and her wallet and other items. A crowd was ahead of us and I didn't like how crowded it was. I moved off of the sidewalk and walked in the street. She walked through the crowd. Along the way, one man held up postcards while someone else stole her camera. . Thieves are quick. They spot valuable items or easy access and you quickly become a target. If you are a keen photographer, certainly take your camera with you. But be cognizant of it at all times. Make some days tourist days and other days photography days. In all my travels, and hearing from many other women who travel, I've only known a couple who were victims of thieves. I've yet to hear of anyone I know personally that has been physically attacked. While I hope you are never put in a position that threatens your safety, the fact is there may come a time when you may have to fight for your life and those you love.*
>
> *Always trust your gut. Move out of a situation that makes you uncomfortable.*

Your main goal is to make it as difficult as possible for thieves or attackers and to enjoy your travels knowing that you have prepared for various scenarios.

After all that information concerning safety, you may become fearful at the thought of travel. Don't be!

As stated by D.J. Bean, "I can think of no more confining or dangerous box than the one whose sides are made of 'It can't happen here.' And whose lid consists of 'It can't/won't happen to me.'"

Can bad things happen? Certainly. Yet they can happen in your own home. In your own city. In your own country.

Chances are they won't happen. You can't let fear stop you from traveling the world.

Use common sense.

Take basic precautions.

Be prepared.

These steps aren't unlike any that you wouldn't do in your own home or city to stay safe.

Emergency Numbers
(Primarily Latin Language Foundation)

Country	Dial	"I need help"
Australia	112	I need help
Austria	112/ 122	Ich brauche Hilfe
Bahamas	911	I need help
Bali	112/118	saya membutuhkan bantuan
Barbados	112	I need help
Belgium	112	Ich brauche Hilfe
Belize	911	I need help
Bermuda	911	I need help
Brazil	190	eu preciso de ajuda
British Virgin Islands	999	I need help
Bulgaria	166	Ich brauche Hilfe
Canada	911	I need help
Canary Islands	112	necesito ayuda
Cayman Islands	999	I need help

Chile	133	necesito ayuda
Colombia	112	necesito ayuda
Costa Rica	128	necesito ayuda
Croatia	112	trebam pomoć
Cuba	999	necesito ayuda
Czech Republic	158	potřebuji pomoci
Denmark	(+45) 112	jeg har brug for hjælp
Dominican Republic	911	necesito ayuda
Easter Island	100-244	necesito ayuda
Ecuador	101	necesito ayuda
El Salvador	993	necesito ayuda
England	999	I need help
Estonia	110	ma vajan abi
Fiji	911	I need help
Finland	112	tarvitsen apua
France	112, 17	j'ai besoin d'aide
Germany	112	Ich brauche Hilfe
Guatemala	110	necesito ayuda
Hungary	112	segítségre van szükségem

Iceland	112	ég þarf hjálp
Ireland, Republic of	112	Teastaíonn cúnamh uaim
Italy	112	ho bisogno di aiuto
Jamaica	119	I need help
Kenya	993	Nahitaji msaada
Lativa	112	man vajag palīdzību
Lithuania	112	man reikia pagalbos
Luxembourg	112	j'ai besoin d'aide
Maldives Republic	119	I need help
Malta	112	għandi bżonn l-għajnuna
Mexico	60	necesito ayuda
Monaco	112	j'ai besoin d'aide
Netherlands	112	ik heb hulp nodig
New Zealand	111	I need help
Northern Ireland	112	Teastaíonn cúnamh uaim

Norway	112	jeg trenger hjelp
Panama	104	necesito ayuda
Paraguay	912	necesito ayuda
Peru	119	necesito ayuda
Philippines	117	kailangan ko ng tulong
Poland	999	potrzebuję pomocy
Portugal	112	eu preciso de ajuda
Puerto Rico	911	necesito ayuda
Romania	112	am nevoie de ajutor
Rwanda	local only	j'ai besoin d'aide
Scotland	112	feumaidh mi cuideachadh
Slovak Republic	158	potrebujem pomoc
Slovenia	113	rabim pomoč
South Africa (Cape town)	10111	I need help
Spain	61	necesito ayuda
Sweden	112	jag behöver hjälp

Trinidad & Tobago	999	I need help
Turkey	100	yardıma ihtiyacım var
Uganda	999	I need help
United Kingdom	112	I need help
United States	911	I need help
Us Virgin Islands	911	I need help
Zimbabwe	999	I need help

Practice the wording in the language of the country you are visiting. For those languages that are difficult for you or are written where you are not able to translate or say it, listen to them through an online translator and then write it down phonetically.

For instance, in South Korean, "I need help" translates to doum-i pil-yohae. Phonetically that may sound like poo-me-p-d-ay. So listen to the words and write it down next to the number in a way that you can easily recall.

Write it down so you will have it such your phone be broken or taken.

In addition, learning key phrases in the language go a long way in any country. Simple manners include learning phrases like please, thank you, excuse me along basic niceties such as hello, goodbye, etc.

Respect the culture and the country. In many places across the globe, they may speak your language, but it is not an excuse to not prepare to try and speak the country's language.

Country	Dial	"I need help"
Cambodia	117	ញុំត្រូវការជំនួយ
China	110	我需要幫助
Cyprus	112	χρειάζομαι βοήθεια
Egypt	122	انا بحاجة الى مساعدة
Ethiopia	91	እርዳታ እፈልጋለሁ
Greece	112	χρειάζομαι βοήθεια
Hong Kong	999	我需要帮助
India	100	मुझे मदद की ज़रूरत है
Israel	100	אני צריך עזרה
Japan	110	私は助けが必要です
Jordan	192	انا بحاجة الى مساعدة
South Korea	112	도움이 필요해.
Macedonia	92	ми треба помош
Morocco	19	انا بحاجة الى مساعدة
Nepal	100	मलाई सहयोग चाहियो
Russia	102	Мне нужна помощь
Singapore	999	我需要帮助

Sri Lanka	118	මට උදව් අවශ්‍යයි
Taiwan	110	我需要幫助
Thailand	191	ฉันต้องการความช่วยเหลือ
Tunisia	197	انا بحاجة الى مساعدة
Ukraine	2	мені потрібна допомога
United Arab Emirates	999	انا بحاجة الى مساعدة

Chapter Six

Health

One of the most critical areas where preparation is required is with your health. You don't want to come down with an illness before or after your trip. Most health concerns during your trip often have to do with digestive issues due to food or water-borne pathogens but becoming ill on trips does happen. You don't want to spend your week in Rome stuck in bed or your vacation in Mexico next to a toilet.

Before the Trip

Increase your immune system by taking your favorite immune booster. If you're into herbal remedies, including ashwagandha powder in smoothies or green drinks will aid with strengthening your immunity. If you are used to taking tinctures, try astragalus or echinacea.

Take or increase your Vitamin C, B vitamins, Vitamin D and other immunity-boosting vitamins. Minerals such as zinc are also important.

When you're traveling you will be out of your time zone and in most cases, be doing a lot of physical activity. If you're not used to walking daily or climbing lots of stairs, get outside and increase your stamina.

Do you have any serious health issue? Ensure that you have enough of the prescription medications that you will need for the duration of your trip. You might want to have some extra but ensure all bottles are labeled. Also be careful of bringing any that could be considered by authorities as opioids that could be sold on the black market. Also, have a written prescription from a doctor.

You may find that your period starts or comes unexpectedly. While similar languages such as English, French and Spanish may be able to help you, other languages (unless that's your first language or you have learned that language) will be harder to decipher such as Mandarin or Russian. See examples below.

English: menstrual pads
French: coussinets menstruels
Spanish: almohadillas menstruales

Chinese: 月经垫 Yuèjīng diàn

Russian: менструальные прокладки
menstrual'nyye prokladki
English: tampon
French: l' tampon
Spanish: el tampón
Chinese: 棉塞 Mián sāi
Russian: тампон tampon

Therefore, learn the words, write them down or ensure you have a way to translate items that you may require. Before your flight, gather up your pre-flight health items.

Essential oils have gained in huge popularity within the last few years and there's a good reason—they work. They may have different names such as Thieves, OnGuard or ImmunityBoost but this is one oil that is great to use for disinfecting and in combination with a vapor rub if ill. Gargling with it can also stop any other germs. Peppermint is good for headaches and stomach aches.

Everyone has their favorite headache or pain remedy, but it's hard to beat the simple aspirin. Carrying aspirin can be useful with a heart attack so good to have on hand in any case.

Homeopathic remedies for cold, flu and other illnesses are easy to carry in your luggage for extra peace of mind.

What are your go-to items to keep in your medicinal kit?

> *Author's Note*
>
> *While I prefer a non-petroleum based product, many are familiar with vapor rubs. There are organic brands you can use or make your own. It's also good to have this in your medicine kit if you come down with any respiratory problem while traveling. Put on your chest and your feet and it can help tremendously. In Rome, I came down with a horrible chest cold. Whether it was from the airplane or from the unaccustomed smoking in many areas such as the subway, I knew I had to stop it. Vapor rub coupled with Thieves essential oil on my chest and feet along with the homeopathic remedy Oscilloccinum saved my trip. I won't go on any trip without those three items in my travel kit.*

Now that you're packed, another consideration is your hands. For those individuals who work with their hands, there are products called invisible gloves. They form a protective barrier with your hands. This is important as what you touch will not attach to your skin. However, one simple remedy is to wash your hands with soap and to not touch your face.

This is easier said than done as we may have a tendency toward rubbing our eyes, nose, etc. The more you can use a tissue or not touch these areas, the greater your changes of not introducing bacteria or a virus through your eyes, nose or mouth. Additionally, don't forget your ear canals. Don't stick your fingers in your ears if they get plugged. Yawn, check gum, drink some water, but try not to introduce any bacteria into the ear canal which is a warm path down to your nasal passages and throat.

If you have difficulty with cabin pressure or you are traveling with a younger child, ear planes are a simple yet effective solution to minimize pain and discomfort.

During Your Travels

In many, if not most cases, you will travel by airplane. The plane is one of the most germ-filled spaces you will encounter on your travels. Recycled air does not help nor the fact that you cannot prevent others from coughing, sneezing or "sharing' any illness they may have. To mitigate catching anything on your flight, there are a few things you can do.

As you prepare for your trip put a small amount of vapor rub around your nostrils. Bacteria gets trapped and it is nice for breathing. On board the plane or train, wipe down the armrests, seatbelt buckle, tray tables, screens or buttons, anything that others have touched.

Keep your airways from getting dried out by adding some essential oils to a small amount of water. You can pick ones for relaxation such as lavender or one to wake you up such as lemon or peppermint.

Sleep is important to not getting ill, but it's difficult to sleep while traveling. Try to take flights that have you arriving as early as possible in the day. If you are taking a train, metro or walking to where you're staying, it will help you conquer jet lag. There is a homeopathic pill that you can take for jet lag during your plane trip. If you drag or feel jet lag, grab a coffee or caffeinated drink.

However, the best way to keep it at bay is getting outdoors and walking. A short nap has often been said as something to avoid but even fifteen to thirty minutes may be enough to carry you through until bedtime.

It's not uncommon to get some leg swelling, either on a plane from sitting so long or depending on the weather and your activities. During your plane ride, keep drinking lots of water. Stretch your legs by walking around, doing ankle circles and not wearing any constricting clothing. You can also take nettle tablets or bring along nettle tea bags for use on your trip. Nettle is a wonderful herb that not only rids the body of excess fluid but is analgesic so that it helps with muscle aches and pains.

While swollen legs or feet may be uncomfortable, the issue of deep vein thrombosis (DVT) can be deadly. For longer trips, it is advised to wear compression socks that aid with circulation. DVT may be evident if you feel pain in your leg, there is a red spot, often under your knee area on your calf and it can feel warm or hot to the touch. For longer flights, you might want to take a couple of aspirin before your flight which may help to thin your blood and assist with preventing blood clots. Again, the best thing is to avoid longer flights if possible and to move around often. Wear compression socks.

Carry a sufficient number of snacks. Better to have more that you won't use or that you can share, then not enough. You want to have snacks that provide sustenance and energy so protein bars, trail mix, or nuts are always good choices. Chocolate also releases serotonin for when those times you're informed your flight is delayed and you're stuck on the plane or in the concourse. Nut butters are also good. Candies and strong peppermints are good to have on hand for low sugar or if a headache or stomach ache is taking hold.

Of course, with any health advice, seek out the expertise of your primary medical doctor for the best course of action for your body.

On Arrival

Health also includes your mental and emotional health. While we want to cram in as much as possible, that mindset can often be detrimental to your enjoyment of the trip.

Yes, you only have a short time in Paris or Rome or where-ever you're heading. But allow for some downtime every day. Often this can be during times when you are traveling from one city to another. This is a time for you to recharge, to relax, to ensure that you're aren't simply checking off boxes.

Are you an early bird? Why not get up and take a walk around the neighborhood, enjoying listening to the world as it wakes from slumber.

Are you a night owl? You'll get a different impression of the city and its culture after the sun goes down.

Some of the best adventures and memories can be found by simply strolling the streets or going window shopping. Stop in at a sidewalk café and enjoy watching people go about their day.

> *Author's Note*
>
> *I've traveled quite a bit and the memories that always stand out to me are not the museums or monuments, it's been the moments.*
>
> *Speaking to a gentleman who was one of the children who was sent away on trains during the bombings of London in the war.*
>
> *Listening to a cold war Russian officer tell about the history that took place where you stand.*
>
> *Enjoying a simple meal of bread, cheese, olives and wine while gazing out at the Mediterranean Sea. Stumbling upon a movie scene being shot while out walking the city.*
>
> *Chatting with a couple whose son is in your hometown while you're in there's.*
>
> *Having the barista at the local coffeeshop, who's only known you for days, say, "Your usual?"*
>
> *Always include downtime. Engage with the locals. Savor the moments.*

Food and drink are areas that tend to cause travelers some of their worst issues.

Carrying a sturdy water bottle is important as you will want to stay hydrated. Plus, it comes in handy as a defense item when full. Becoming dehydrated can cause headaches, fatigue and more issues with jet lag, and other ailments. Know where you are traveling and if you can drink the water. Even in developed countries, the water will differ from what you are used to drinking. This can even happen in traveling in the states from one city to another city. Use a water bottle or straw that has a filter in it. Don't forget the ice which will melt into your other drink and could cause you some issues. In places where you're either unsure of the water or they have advised you not to drink the water, remember that this will include rinsing your mouth after brushing your teeth.

One of the first signs that you may a bacterial infection is often diarrhea. Even for you women that are past the need for pads on a monthly basis would be well advised to carry a few in case you become ill because of food or water-borne contamination. Often it can strike quickly, and you may not be able to access a bathroom right away. This can save your underwear and maybe even your dignity. If diarrhea strikes, as counter-intuitive as it seems, you will want to add fiber to your diet right away. The fiber will help bulk up your stools so that you don't move into phase two where you come down with flu-like symptoms of chills and fever. Allow the diarrhea to move through your system, usually, twenty-four hours is sufficient and then you can add in the fiber.

In addition to fiber, you'll want to ensure that you replace your electrolytes from any diarrhea or vomiting, There are electrolyte powders you can carry in your medicine kit which make it easy to drink at the first sign of illness. If you forgot or ran out, you can make a simple electrolyte help until you can get to a store.

Combine a sugar source (approximately two tablespoons of sugar or two teaspoons of honey) with sea salt (Himalayan or similar salt will provide you with trace minerals.) Mix them together and add to eight ounces of water along with lemon or orange juice (a quarter to half a cup). You can even grab some lemon juice packets at fast food type establishments or get a container of lemon juice from the local grocer and keep in your room. In the best case scenario, you will simply use it to enhance your water, add to your tea, or use on your hair for sun-kissed highlights.

Should you become ill, kefir or yogurt will settle your stomach and help introduce good bacteria back into your gut. Bananas are a great source of potassium. Other foods that help with calcium, magnesium and potassium are avocadoes, spinach, nuts like almonds and cashews or legumes like peanuts. This can help alleviate any leg cramps as well.

It's often advised to avoid raw foods, or things that may be undercooked, etc. Take precautions but don't allow too much stringency so that you become afraid to eat or try anything. Many grocery stores will sell produce cleaners, or you can also soak fruits and vegetables in apple cider vinegar. This may not obliterate any problems with unwashed produce, but it can mitigate many simple issues of cleanliness.

After a day of walking ten or more miles through museums or other places or climbing many flights of steps, a nice bath or foot bath with Epsom salts will alleviate any aches or pains. Being on your feet all day can supply you not only with sore feet but hot spots, blisters and other ailments. If you will be doing lots of walking, purchase shoes a half-size up or that has adequate space in your toe box to prevent rubbing and that allows swelling in your feet. If you are wearing socks with shoes, choose a wool or other moisture-wicking sock and wear a lightweight inner sock. This will prevent blisters from forming. If you do get a blister or hot spot, use a product called 'second skin' which aids when you have any issues on your feet as it alleviates pressure and irritation while helping with healing.

Depending on the time of year, you may find that you are dealing with very different weather patterns. In some countries around the globe, air conditioning is not always available. Heat stroke is a serious issue.

Here are the symptoms of heat stroke:

- Headache
- Feeling lightheaded, dizzy
- Not sweating, clammy
- Hot, dry and red skin

Most often this is because of dehydration and drinking water will help. Note that you do not want to

drink ice cold water. This will aggravate the headache and other symptoms. It is best to drink cool or room temperature water.

If you experience any of these additional symptoms, you need to seek immediate attention. These include:

- Cramps or muscle weakness
- Nausea
- Vomiting
- Rapid heartbeat
- Rapid and shallow breathing (unable to 'catch' your breath)
- Behavior changes (feeling confused, disoriented, staggering)

Many of the symptoms associated with heat stroke can also

occur with altitude sickness. People who are from a lower altitude can also experience many of these symptoms. Dehydration is also a major

factor.

Without getting help, heat stroke and altitude sickness can lead to seizures, becoming unconscious and in the worst scenario, death.

Hypothermia occurs when the body gets too cold. Wearing appropriate clothing and finding shelter if the weather changes dramatically will be critical to preventing a drop in body temperature. In most cases, not being able to think properly and behavior changes will signal that help is required.

Accidents and serious illness can occur traveling. In these instances, you will need to seek immediate medical attention. Prepare yourself for this possibility by carrying on your person the following:

1) Travel insurance documentation
2) Your information (name, date of birth, etc.)
3) Vitals: blood type, any prescriptions you are on, and any known allergies
4) Contact in case of emergency

Note that you want to carry this "on your person" so in a neck pouch or waist wallet, etc. as your purse or other bag may not be on your person when the accident occurs.

TRAVEL MORE. TRAVEL WELL. TRAVEL SOON.

Notes

Chapter Seven

Packing

Nine times out of ten you'll leave at least a third of your items you've packed untouched. You know, those things that you packed "just in case." With charges for luggage, packing light will not only save you from hauling a huge bag around but will save you money.

There are three areas to cover in packing. First, your clothing, next is your technology and third, cash on hand.

Clothing and Jewelry

Pick a color scheme and stick with it. One to two base colors and one accent color or pattern will provide enough options for changing up your daily attire. Additionally, it frees up your luggage to purchase some clothing or shoes abroad.

If traveling during times of seasonal change, think layers. A wrap or light sweater is something that can often be used all year round. A large wrap can be used as a blanket or pillow when traveling or for cover. It can be used as a cover-up at the beach or pool. It can be tied to create a quick holder for food purchases.

During the winter or seasonal months, a jacket with a zip-out liner is not too heavy and can be used when it's rainy or windy outdoors. Adding a heavier sweater underneath along with gloves and a hat may be all that you require to travel in winter.

If you are checking a bag, keep another set of lingerie and a large t-shirt in your purse or backpack. Then if they lose your luggage, you still have a set of clean underwear and something to sleep in during the night. If you're wearing pants and a top, you could also bring another top.

You should keep jewelry to a minimum and not bring or wear any of your favorite items. Wearing costume or simple jewelry discourages thieves and you don't worry about losing your favorite earrings or leaving a ring behind at the last place you stayed.

Good shoes are vital to enjoying your trip. Before you go on any trip that requires a lot of walking (which are most trips), you want to have shoes that have been broken in. You want to ensure that any shoes you take are comfortable and don't rub. Those shoes you've had for a year that worked great last year—don't wear them. Buy a pair like them. Bring shoes that work with most, if not all, of your outfits. Pick your shoes on what you're planning on doing during your trip.

Traveling light allows for less concern with keeping track of your bags and more ability to take public transportation. Plus, now you have room to bring home those great shoes you bought.

> *Author's Note*
>
> *I didn't heed my own advice on a short trip and wore a ring that held special memories for me from a previous trip. Somewhere while traveling, it slipped off of my finger. I think it probably happened when I dried my hands over the bin. But I was in a hurry as the flight would be boarding soon. I didn't realize until later that it was missing. Of course, this could happen anywhere, but I could possibly go back to those areas around where I live. It was a hard lesson that I had to remember what jewelry to wear on trips.*

Technology

Technology can be useful, but it can also be detrimental. Use your technology wisely but don't allow it to distract from taking time to focus on where you're at in that moment. The more you connect with your device for advice, the less you interact with people. To get a true sense of place, you will need to connect with its population. Yes, you can find a restaurant online but why not ask someone on the street to recommend their favorite place?

Decide how much technology you need to carry with you. Today's mobile phones are basically computers in their own right. You can use them for entertainment, for taking photos, for directions, for adding in written or spoken notes, etc.

A printed book won't run out of batteries and won't be desirable for thieves. Unless you'll be working while away from home, it limits the need for a laptop or even a tablet. Many hotels, bed and breakfasts, and other establishments will have computers. Why lug around a heavy item that you don't need? It's also a good time to take stock of how much you feel the need for such devices.

Often the main thing that people want to know is how to stay in touch with family or friends while abroad. There are many applications that you can download on your phone or tablet to assist with this. Some people enjoy apps like WhatsApp while others use Skype or similar tools. Because new applications are always arriving or apps are changed, this is an area to do your research.

You can also get a global communication plan through your phone carrier if you feel that is necessary. However, before purchasing, make sure that the plan will work in the country or region where you are traveling.

If you are working while traveling, you may need to have your laptop with you. As with other vital information, have everything saved to a cloud storage. Do not put any information that could cause you harm on your computer if it should be mislaid or stolen. Consider travel insurance for it.

> *Author's Note*
>
> *One of the best thing that ever happened to me was my phone wouldn't work while traveling in London. Before one outing I had looked at a map before I left for the day. I knew the area I would visit for the day and wanted to go to the Victoria and Albert museum. I'd noted landmarks but the actual location was difficult to see any landmarks. So, I had to go ask a group of workers which way to head. These guys were friendly and helpful. As I made my way in the direction they pointed, I stumbled upon a college. In the green, they had a big open-air food event going on. The smells were delicious and while it tempted me, I wanted to get to the museum which was a good thing as you could spend days, if not weeks there. Not once did I feel afraid or 'without' because my phone GPS wasn't working. In fact, it freed me—an introvert—to stop and connect with people, even if it was simply to ask directions. Technology is good but it is also insulating. That day taught me that.*

Cash versus Credit

We've become a credit society. Even if you don't use credit cards, you may use a debit card in place of cash or check. When traveling, you will want to have cash in that country's currency and in a variety of lower denominations. You also don't want to pay fees. At much as possible, use a card that charges no ATM or cash withdrawal fees or foreign transaction fees.

While you can get the currency at the airport, the charges are often higher. If you can get currency before your trip, it's better. However, you will want to have enough local money when you arrive at your new destination. Why not wait until you get there? Because you may find you need some coinage or cash before you can access a currency exchange or automatic teller machine.

At the airport or train station find an ATM and take out enough money until you get to your next destination. There's nothing more fun than finding out that no one will accept a credit card and you can't find a place to get cash.

While we are used to being able to use the toilet without paying, in many countries or certain facilities, you will have to pay to access the restrooms. Having a small amount of local currency will ensure that you can use the facilities and still catch your train before it departs.

In the case of theft, prepare to have cash stashed in different places. As noted, hidden pockets in coats or vests, a neck or waist pouch are worth consideration. Some people have even suggested a fake wallet that you carry with you. Only put in enough money for that day. You can put in some pretend cards in the slots. If someone steals it or asks you to hand over your wallet, you can give them the decoy. It can save you from handing over your real wallet with your credit cards, any information concerning you, and other cash.

Learn the currency as much as you can before you go. Know what the exchange rate is as this will help to keep you on budget while traveling.

With packing the adage holds true. Pack less clothes, Take more money.

Author's Note

I prefer to pack light but I'm not a minimalist by any means. On a trip to France and the UK for approximately three weeks, I took my big purse and one carry-on. This was during the fall, so I took a jacket that had a removable liner. The thing about packing light is especially important if you are traveling solo. With larger bags or more than one bag, your focus is on your luggage and often your hands are full. You want to keep your hands free so that you don't become an easy target for someone. When you travel by public transportation, this also means lugging bags up and down stairs. Even a smaller bag becomes heavy when you're going up long flights of stairs.

Pack light. You'll be happier and it frees you up to enjoy yourself. No one cares you wear the same outfit more than once.

More Travel Tips

- Determine what you want to do when you travel. If want to explore museums or shop, then you will be indoors most of the time, so it doesn't matter if it is cold and snowy or hot and humid outdoors. If you plan on exploring the countryside or gardens, then you'll want to come in spring or early fall depending on the areas you wish to explore.
- For better discounts and less congestion with lots of people, take your trips in the off-season.
- Consider your currency against where you are traveling. The currency being in your favor will allow you to spend less if your currency is at a better rate than the country you are visiting.
- Plan your trip as early in advance as possible and prepare a projected budget of anticipated expenses. This will allow you to save for the trip while also using ways to gain miles and points through credit cards or airline shopping portals.
- Always purchase as much as possible through shopping portals or other avenues that provide you with incentives, points or miles. You don't have to have a credit card to use these portals, but if you use the credit card of that portal, you can easily double or triple your miles or points.
- When making any hotel or lodging reservations, make sure that you are making them for the day of arrival. Check your transportation tickets! You may gain or lose a day depending on your travel and could end up losing your reservation.

- When traveling to more than one city, fly into one city and fly out of the last city that you visit. Fly into the city that supplies the best offering for cost and convenience.
- Consider airport fees and taxes when using points or miles. Fly into or out of airports with the least amount of taxes or fees attached to miles or points.
- The lighter that you pack, the easier it will be to use public transportation, regional airlines or trains. Unless you will be on a boat or staying in one hotel the entire time, try to combine all your luggage requirements into one carry-on.
- Choose activities that include food or drink as part of the activity such as a cooking class, wine-tasting, chocolate making, cheese tour, etc.
- For clothing, create a capsule wardrobe with one primary neutral color (blue, brown, black, tan), one secondary color (cream, maroon, red) and one tertiary color or pattern that includes the other colors.
- Choose your wardrobe colors in relation to where you are traveling. European countries tend to wear more neutrals such as browns, blacks and tans, while other countries such as some African or Asian countries like India or South American countries like Mexico are known for bright, vivid colors.

About the Author

Vikki Walton is a global traveler who is also the founder of girlswantago. She enjoys visiting other countries and cultures and is a slow traveler in that she often housesits when traveling. You can often find her traveling solo, with her daughters, Michelle and Jori, or with friends. In addition to traveling, Vikki is an author of the vocational guidance book, Work Quilting and a cozy mystery backyard farming series.

You can connect with her through:

www.VikkiWalton.com

https://www.facebook.com/VikkiWaltonAuthor/

www.girlswantago.com

https://www.facebook.com/Girlswantago/

Travel More, Travel Well, Travel Soon.

My Travel Plans To:

Date/s:

Country/Region:

Places I want to visit:

Things I want to do:

Items I want to eat/drink/try:

Highlights of my trip would be:

My Trip Theme

If you are traveling with others, have them give input on the trip's theme. They can have their own theme, you can have a daily theme, you can have a group theme.

Travel Budget

Total Budget Goal:

- Savings:
- Gifts:
- Miles:
- Points:
- Discounts:
- Cost-sharing:
- Misc.:

Current Total:

Total Needed:

Examples:

- [ ] $200 per day (breakfast, lunch, dinner, activity, transportation and lodging if shared)
- [ ] 25,000 miles for economy, 50,000 business, or 100,000 first class one-way ticket
- [ ] Free hotel night discount after five nights

Ideas for saving or making money for travel

Budget (overall):

Pre-trip costs (passport, Global Entry, luggage, insurance, etc.)
    Thrifty
    Anticipated
    Splurge

Transportation (to destination, during time at destination; class desired--first, business, econ, etc.)
    Thrifty
    Anticipated
    Splurge

Lodging or accommodations (hotel, rental, hostel, etc.)
    Thrifty
    Anticipated
    Splurge

Food and drink (breakfast, lunch, snacks, dinner, desserts, classes, cooking, etc.)
    Thrifty
    Anticipated
    Splurge

Activity costs
    Thrifty
    Anticipated
    Splurge

Miscellaneous expenses
    Thrifty
    Anticipated
    Splurge

Post-trip charges (if any)
    Thrifty
    Anticipated
    Splurge

TOTAL Thrifty
TOTAL Anticipated
TOTAL Splurge

Where I plan to stay

Name:

Address:

City:

Phone number:

Email:

Website:

Reservation Number:

Hotel Chain Membership Number:

Arrival airport:

Distance from airport:

Arrival Train Station:

Distance from train station:

Arrival Bus Station:

Distance from bus station:

Transportation: Airline

Airport Name
Airport Designation (ABC)

- Flight Reservation
- Flight Boards
- Flight Leaves
- Flight Connection
- Flight Boards
- Flight Leaves
- Flight Arrives

Airport Name
Airport Designation (ABC)

- Flight Reservation
- Flight Boards
- Flight Leaves
- Flight Connection
- Flight Boards
- Flight Leaves
- Flight Arrives

Transportation: Train or Bus

Station Name

Station City Designation (ABC)

- Reservation
- Boarding
- Leaves
- Connection
- Boards
- Leaves
- Arrives

Station Name

Station City Designation (ABC)

- Reservation
- Boards
- Leaves
- Connection
- Boards
- Leaves
- Arrives

Notes:

Transportation: Vehicle Rental

Rental Company Name

Rental Company City Designation (ABC)

- Vehicle Reservation
- Vehicle Type
- Vehicle Pickup Date and Time
- Vehicle Gas (Return)
- Vehicle Return Date and Time
- Vehicle Insurance
- Vehicle (options—GPS, etc.)

Rental Company Name

Rental Company City Designation (ABC)

- Vehicle Reservation
- Vehicle Type
- Vehicle Pickup Date and Time
- Vehicle Gas (Return)
- Vehicle Return Date and Time
- Vehicle Insurance
- Vehicle (options—GPS, etc.)

Notes:

Transportation: Boat or Ship

Cruise Name
Positioning City

- Reservation
- Boarding
- Leaves
- Arrives

Cruise Name
Positioning City

- Reservation
- Boarding
- Leaves
- Arrives

Notes:

Activities

Events

City Passes:

Metro/subway Passes:

Activities:

1.
2.
3.
4.
5.
6.
7.
8.
9.
10.

Itinerary

Quad 1

Quad 2

Quad 3

Quad 4

Quad 5

Quad 6

Quad 7

Quad 8

Quad 9

Quad 10

THINGS TO DO

HOME

WORK

PERSONAL

TRIP/OTHER

First Leg of Trip

Theme:

Date and Day of Departure:

From (city):

Departure Time:

Transportation mode:

Date and Day of Arrival:

To (city):

Lodging:

- o Name
- o Address
- o Location in City
- o Shuttle to/from airport
- o Closest Public Transportation
- o Breakfast Included?

Quad 1

Quad 2

Quad 3

Quad 4

Quad 5

Second Leg of Trip

Theme:

Date and Day of Departure:

From (city):

Departure Time:

Transportation mode:

Date and Day of Arrival:

From (city):

Lodging:

- o Name
- o Address
- o Location in City
- o Shuttle to/from airport
- o Closest Public Transportation
- o Breakfast Included?

Quad 1

Quad 2

Quad 3

Quad 4

Quad 5

Third Leg of Trip

Date and Day of Departure:

From (city):

Departure Time:

Transportation mode:

Date and Day of Arrival:

To (city):

Lodging:

- o   Name
- o   Address
- o   Location in City
- o   Shuttle to/from airport
- o   Closest Public Transportation
- o   Breakfast Included?

Quad 1

Quad 2

Quad 3

Quad 4

Quad 5

Fourth Leg of Trip

Date and Day of Departure:

From (city):

Departure Time:

Transportation mode:

Date and Day of Arrival:

To (city):

Lodging:

- o Name
- o Address
- o Location in City
- o Shuttle to/from airport
- o Closest Public Transportation
- o Breakfast Included?

Quad 1

Quad 2

Quad 3

Quad 4

Quad 5

Fifth Leg of Trip

Date and Day of Departure:

From (city):

Departure Time:

Transportation mode:

Date and Day of Arrival:

To (city):

Lodging:

- o Name
- o Address
- o Location in City
- o Shuttle to/from airport
- o Closest Public Transportation
- o Breakfast Included?

Quad 1

Quad 2

Quad 3

Quad 4

Quad 5

Doodles, Insights, Memories

Doodles, Insights, Memories

Doodles, Insights, Memories

Doodles, Insights, Memories

Doodles, Insights, Memories

Doodles, Insights, Memories

Doodles, Insights, Memories

Doodles, Insights, Memories

Doodles, Insights, Memories

Doodles, Insights, Memories

Doodles, Insights, Memories

Doodles, Insights, Memories

www.ingramcontent.com/pod-product-compliance
Lightning Source LLC
Chambersburg PA
CBHW030119100526
44591CB00009B/456